Twenty-First Century Democratic Renaissance

-

From Plato
to
Neoliberalism
to
Planetary Democracy

Errol E Harris

The Institute for Economic Democracy Press

Published by: the Institute for Economic Democracy Press
Sun City, AZ, Fayetteville, PA
888.533.1020 - www.ied.info - ied@ied.info
In Cooperation with the Institute on World Problems
www.worldproblems.net and Earth Rights Institute – www.earthrights.net

Library of Congress Cataloging-in-Publication Data

Harris, Errol E.
 Twenty-first century democratic renaissance : from Plato to neoliberalism to planetary democracy / Errol E Harris.
    p. cm.
 Includes bibliographical references and index.
 ISBN-13: 978-1-933567-15-0 (pbk.)
 ISBN-13: 978-1-933567-14-3 (hbk)

 1. Democracy--Philosophy. 2. Democracy--Philosophy--History. I. Title.
 JC423.H3733 2008
 321.8--dc22   2007046359

Cover: Secondary students of City Montessori School, Lucknow, India, model World Parliament in conformance with a *Constitution for the Federation of Earth* debating legislative proposals within a democratic Earth Federation. City Montessori School, Lucknow, is the laureate of the UNESCO Peace Education Prize of 2002, as well as recipient of numerous other awards for excellent education. It is also in the Guinness Book of Records as the largest private school in a single city, and currently has over 29000 students enrolled at over 25 campuses. The Model World Parliament is a regular, voluntary, practical exercise among interested students at most of the CMS campuses.   www.cmseducation.org

This book is printed on acid free paper.

The Institute for Economic Democracy is dedicated to producing a philosophy for elimination of waste within the economy, that ends poverty, and that provides a quality life for each citizen of earth.

Towards that end we have published the books listed below. For later books go to www.ied.info.

Economic Democracy: A Grand Strategy for Global Peace and Prosperity, 2nd edition, 2008, J.W. Smith

Money: A Mirror Image of the Economy, 2nd edition, 2008, J.W. Smith

The Earth Belongs to Everyone, 2008, Alanna Hartzok

Ascent to Freedom: The Philosophical Foundations of Democratic World Law, 2007, Glen T. Martin

Millennium Dawn: The Philosophy of Planetary Crisis and Human Liberation, 2005, Glen T. Martin

World Revolution Through World Law: Basic Documents of the Emerging Earth Federation, 2006, Glen T. Martin

Earth Federation Now! Tomorrow is Too Late, 2005. Errol E. Harris

Economic Democracy: The Political Struggle of the Twenty-First Century, 4th edition, 2005, J.W. Smith

WHY: The Deeper History of the September 11th Terrorist Attack on America, 3rd edition, 2005, J.W. Smith

Cooperative Capitalism: A Blueprint for Global Peace and Prosperity, 2nd edition, 2005, J.W. Smith

A Constitution for the Federation of Earth, Editor Glen T. Martin

Emerging World Law, Editors Eugenia Almand and Glen T. Martin

ii

Foreword

Glen T. Martin

Professor of Philosophy, Radford University
Author, *Ascent to Freedom – Practical and Philosophical Foundations
of Democratic World Law*

Democratic thought, as Professor Harris ably shows, has a long history reaching back to the ancient Greek thinkers. Plato clearly understood that government must be premised on reasoned dialogue, moderation, and a vision of the common good. His pupil Aristotle developed an ethical and political philosophy revealing human beings as "rational animals" and very widely capable of achieving practical wisdom (*phronesis*), virtue, and happiness. Democratic theory as it was subsequently developed over the centuries took as its most fundamental premise these common features of our humanity and our human potential.

It is this understanding of both our universal potential and its necessarily social character that underlies modern democratic theory at its best. In many ways, these ancient insights come to fruition in the profound articulations of democratic theory found in such thinkers as Immanuel Kant, G.W.F. Hegel, T.H. Green, Bernard Bosanquet, Earnest Barker, and Jürgen Habermas. Professor Harris treats of all of these thinkers except Habermas, illuminating, in the process, the dynamics of mature democracy. He shows clearly their common understanding of the profoundly social character of human reasoning, understanding, and freedom. Without a democratic institutional matrix that enhances free communication and discussion, our highest human potentialities for rationality, productive cooperation, and ethical self-realization will necessarily atrophy.

Habermas' democratic theory adds little to the concept of the institutional matrix suggested by the other thinkers identified here. This matrix must involve a free press, freedom of thought and speech, and institutionalized public spaces where authentic dialogue and debate can develop among citizen participants. Habermas' theory does, however, contribute an empirical and social-scientific justification to democratic theory that was largely only intuited by the earlier thinkers in this tradition. For he shows that the basic principles of communicative thought, dialogue, and ethical reciprocity lie at the heart of language itself. Language may well be the most universal defining feature of our common humanity. And at the heart of every language, drawn upon by every competent speaker of a language, are the fundamental criteria for human institutions premised on democracy, freedom, and equality.

Noted linguist and renowned political commentator Noam Chomsky routinely expresses his faith in the common sense and wisdom of ordinary people. If practical reason appears to be blocked in ordinary citizens, this may well be due to economic, commercial, and political institutions that substitute propaganda and social conditioning for genuine discussion and debate. It may well be due to irrational institutions like the sovereign nation-state that fragment humanity into warring, militarized national units based on fear, propaganda, and secrecy, rather than mutual trust, dialogue, and openness. Chomsky's political commentaries routinely point out these deleterious effects of contemporary political culture and its institutional settings.

As Professor Harris shows, it is this common sense and this capacity to develop practical wisdom that is denied by the tradition that evolved through Nazi legal theorist Carl Schmitt, Joseph Schumpeter, Vilfredo Pareto, Friedrich von Hayek, Hans Morgenthau, and Leo Strauss. These thinkers seriously misunderstand legitimate government under distorted ideas of a Hobbesian struggle for naked power and, in doing so, pave the way for totalitarianism with its irrational systems of domination and exploitation. However, the contemporary world, reeling under the destructive consequences of their thought, is by no means without hope for a genuine Democratic Renaissance.

With unerring insight, Professor Harris puts his finger on the greatest institutional impediment to realizing the promise of democracy and freedom on Earth – the system of sovereign nation-states itself. Under today's global crises – including global warming, resource depletion, pollution, militarism, terrorism, and weapons of mass destruction – nation-states have lost the traditional rational justifications for their existence as democracies: the rule of equitably enforced law and promotion of the common good of citizens. The system of militarized sovereign nations today blocks the further realization of authentic democracy on Earth and violates the potential unity and natural sympathies of our common humanity.

Harris shows in his final chapter in what ways the actualization of worldwide democracy through a carefully designed Earth Federation can deal effectively with our seemingly insoluble global crises of environmental destruction, militarism, war, and global terrorism. It is democracy itself, with its inherent potential actualized and universalized, that provides the real hope for the future of humankind. In a bare 150 pages, this little volume presents a clear and cogent expression, not only of the essence of democratic thought, but of the way forward beyond our presently endangered future. Harris' reasoning here is pragmatic, common sense, and carefully developed. That way forward is premised on the universalization of democratic rationality, cooperation, and freedom in the form of a non-military, democratic Earth Federation.

Table of Contents

Twenty-first Century Democratic Renaissance

From Plato
to
Neoliberalism
to
Planetary Democracy

Introduction

The rational nature that distinguishes humanity from other species of animal impels all thinking people to reflect upon their way of life and to seek to improve it. The ultimate human quest is to discover the best way of living, and as human beings are by nature social, this quest involves the endeavor to determine the best kind of social order. Since the beginnings of western culture in the civilization of Ancient Greece, people have found it impossible to achieve satisfaction under conditions of servitude and duress, and they have, therefore, pursued the ideal of personal freedom, to be attained through individual conduct and attitude concurrently with the appropriate social and political organization. As this enterprise has developed in the course of history, a general consensus has emerged that the only form of political structure that will assure freedom is democracy, so that in recent times even totalitarian regimes have advertised themselves as forms of democracy (as, for instance, the "people's democracy" of China, and since they operate as dictatorships they excuse this form of government as dictatorship of the proletariat.

The appeal of democracy, as the best form of social structure, has sound rational grounds. Human beings cannot live in solitude; at birth they are helpless, needing fostering by their parents, and thereafter they are dependent on the co-operation of, and intercommunication with, their fellows. It follows that their natural and normal way of life is social, the common life of a society which has to be regulated so that anarchy and conflict are avoided; and the rules must be known to all and enforced upon the recalcitrant. Ordered social living requires some form of government. But nobody is content to submit to the arbitrary will of another, and as submission to some superior authority is unavoidable, a way must be found to ensure that the imposed will is not unacceptable.

Rulers are apt to govern in their own interests at the expense of their subjects, with some degree of oppression and injustice as a result; and, even when despots or oligarchs are benevolent, it is left to them to decide what is best for their subordinates: a decision that is always more or less arbitrary, even when they consult reputed sages. When it is least so there will always be some who disagree and resent what they feel to be oppressive. What will satisfy any person can ultimately be decided only by that person and freedom of choice, even though the choice may initially be mistaken, is the only way to assure final contentment, for we can learn what will satisfy us only by experience. Even Plato's doctrine that those should govern who are best qualified and who know best what is for the good of all – that philosophers should be kings – fails, because even philosophers disagree and, in the absence of Plato, the decision as to what is best for the people cannot be reliably decided unless the people themselves are consulted.

Whatever difficulties may attend the practice, therefore, the best way to achieve popular contentment seems to be to allow the people who are subject to government to rule themselves, either directly or by delegation of power, and to ensure that government is conditional upon the consent of the governed.

Throughout the centuries philosophers have developed theories of the nature of democracy that have established a tradition recognizing fundamental rights of persons and a general structure of political institutions designed to assert and protect those rights. The prevailing form of political regime throughout the world at the present time is one that professes to be democratic. Even military dictatorships tend to declare themselves temporary as the means to avert especially critical emergencies, with the eventual intention of "restoring democracy." And those that are communistic claim the title because they profess to be ruling in the interests of the mass of the people – the proletariat. Marxists, who explain all social and political practice in terms of the means of economic production adopted by society, maintain that capitalistic regimes are not really democratic, in the full sense, because the capitalists (the *bourgeoisie*) exploit and oppress the workers who remain ground down in poverty. If democracy, they argue, is the rulership of the people and the proletariat constitutes the mass of the people, then the government should be in their hands; hence genuine democracy must be a communistic dictatorship representing the proletariat – it is a dictatorship only until all political rule has been converted into administration and the state has withered away altogether. The French Revolution, they contend, was a bourgeois revolution, transferring power from the nobility to the capitalistic *bourgeoisie*, who then exploited the poverty of the working class for their own benefit.

The theories have in part professed to be descriptive and in part have essayed to be normative and prescriptive, and questions naturally arise how far theory reflects practice and to what extent practice conforms to the norms set by the theorists. The tradition that has evolved sets out an ideal of democracy which contemporary politicians tend to claim is approximated in the structure and practice of the states whose affairs they administer. It will be the purpose of the study which follows to examine this claim.

I shall remind my reader of the way the idea of democracy has developed from the Ancient Greeks to the present day. I shall then examine the practice of democracy in those states which claim to be democratic *par excellence* and are generally recognized as the paradigm cases. These are the regimes that have arisen in Western Europe and those in America and elsewhere that have developed in the European tradition. My object is to assess the practice in the light of the theory and then to consider how far the former conforms, or fails to conform, to the latter, how failure to fulfill theoretical ideals endangers our future and how such failure might be remedied. No decision can safely be made about these matters, however, that omits to take into account the vast changes in social and international conditions that have occurred in recent decades. Since the theories under consideration were worked out, enormous crises and world wars have affected political attitudes and have given rise to international institutions that supervene over those that have hitherto existed, and we need to reflect upon the relevance to these of the concept of democracy as well as the effects that they may have produced on this concept itself. Not only were there two devastating World Wars and a major communistic revolution in the early decades of the twentieth century, which left intolerable tension between the rival ideologies of liberal democracy and soviet communism – a cold war that threatened almost daily to erupt into nuclear conflict – weapons of mass destruction having been developed that can wipe out whole populations. The most powerful nations have armed themselves with arsenals sufficient to do precisely that, while many of the less powerful are doing their best to follow suit. In these circumstances war is no longer a tolerable instrument of policy – not even the threat of war because no threat is effective unless it is backed by the actual intention to carry it out. But up to the present the way of preventing war, if there is any, has not been recognized or contemplated by politicians or by any prominent political leader. So the whole world has lived for the past sixty years under the looming threat of total destruction by nuclear and other weapons of incredible destructive power. Not even since the Soviet Union has internally collapsed has this dire threat been removed, because the major powers still retain their arsenals and no way has been found of preventing proliferation among the lesser nations, several of which have already acquired nuclear capability. Scientists have predicted that devastation and fall-out resulting from a nuclear war would not only exterminate the combatants but that the effect on the world's climate would produce a new ice age – a nuclear winter, destructive of civilized life the world over.

Meanwhile, the vast use of fossil fuels in automobiles, aircraft and industries has for decades (or even centuries) been belching out greenhouse gases into the Earth's atmosphere and is causing climate change that, if unchecked, will destroy the delicate balance of meteorological and chemical conditions of air and water that make our planet inhabitable by living beings. The effects have been exacerbated by unchecked and unconscionable destruction of tropical rain forests, the so-called lungs of the Earth which inhale carbon dioxide and exhale oxygen. The effects of this climate change, already apparent and feared by scientists to be irreversible, include increasing desertification, causing failure of crops and unprecedented human famine, as well as the melting of the polar ice-caps and consequent rising of sea levels which will flood coasts on which many of the most populous and important cities of the world are situated and where a large proportion of the world's people now live. It is here also that much of the arable land lies which is cultivated to feed them. Even worse, the increased CO^2 in the air is being dissolved in and is acidifying the oceans, which will make them lethal to plankton, the basis of the food chain throughout the planet. The ozone layer in the upper atmosphere, which protects crops and other living beings, including humans, from lethal cosmic radiation, has been damaged possibly irremediably (although the process of destruction has in this case been checked). Meanwhile, the demands of industrialization complicated by other causes are reducing the water table in many crucial regions of the world, depriving the people of clean drinking water. The result is an impending cause of mass migration of populations, and as several countries draw their water from the same source, severe tension and conflict between neighboring nations threatening further military ventures with unforeseeable consequences.

The causes and advance of climate change are a topic the investigation and discussion of which could fill many volumes, some of which have already been published, perhaps the most telling and moving being *Red Sky at Morning*, by James Gustave Speth, extensive quotation from which, however tempting, is not admissible in the introduction to a discussion such as is being undertaken here, but reference to the book, which should be required reading for all politicians, is strongly to be recommended.

Warfare with weapons of mass destruction and the dire effects of climate change that are continuously increasing unchecked are the two main overarching perils that menace the human race today, and there are many more less ominous but far from insignificant. Without major political changes and reforms humanity is likely to be overwhelmed by these crises, the implications of which cry out for attention and radical action.

The collapse of the Soviet Union towards the close of the last century prompted Francis Fukuyama to announce "the end of history" because, he averred, democracy had now become the universally approved political order. "The story of our history is the story of our ideological evolution; that evolution culminates in liberal democracy"[1] which he identifies with the ideals of the American and French revolutions. Just what these might be he does not elaborate. Although we are all acquainted with the popular slogan, *"liberte, egalite et fraternite"* (a banner under which Terror ruled and thousands of people were condemned to death) we can hardly be confident that it is sufficient to guarantee respect for human rights. As an indication of the ideals of democracy this is at best somewhat tenuous. Moreover, it is far from obvious that the end of the Soviets has ushered in the universal adoption of these ideals; nor is the description of our history as the evolution of ideology wholly convincing. More important, it would be prudent, before assuring ourselves that history had reached its consummation, to inquire whether the democracy that had (assumedly) been universally approved was authentic and genuinely able to deliver the freedom that we all desire — not merely negative freedom from interference and prohibition, but positive freedom to do whatever we think right. Can it deliver a solution to the dire crises that threaten our civilization and the very existence of life on Earth?

During the last century serious criticisms of liberal democracy have been voiced by eminent writers on political science. We need to consider how far the detractions of these critics have been justified, how they may be met if at all, and whether the remedies they advocate are appropriate and acceptable. It is also important to investigate whether and to what extent the influence of such critics has itself been responsible for the erosion of the democratic ideal in our day. We have reason, very different from that alleged by Fukuyama, to fear that the imminent end of human history is indeed the prospect foreshadowed at the present time by the perils of nuclear conflict and environmental deterioration. And, besides evaluating their causes, we must assess those conditions that prevent our removing them. We need to consider whether it is possible to reinvigorate the essential ideals of democracy, and whether, if it is, such reinvigoration may give hope that the tragic denouement can be averted. Is the establishment of democracy world-wide really feasible? Is it possible on the basis of nationally independent sovereign state-hood? Can it offer solutions to the problems facing humanity at the present time? These are the questions the following chapters are intended to address.

Whatever answers may be contemplated, we need not concern ourselves with the end of history, if any such is conceivable; more relevant is the possibility that history will continue; and if, as R.G. Collingwood maintained, history is the record of *res gestae*,[2] this will imply the continuation of human life on this planet and the pervasive physico-chemical conditions that support it.

---

[1] Cf. *The National Interest*, Summer 1989.

[2] Cf. R. G. Collingwood, *The Principles of History*, Eds. W.H. Dray and W.J. van der Dussen (Oxford, Oxford University Press, 1999,2001),p..40.

1. Freedom and the Tradition of Democracy

The statue of Liberty dominates the approach to New York harbor, but just how the French donors of the statue, or the citizens of the newly established United States to whom it was donated, understood the liberty that the statue symbolizes is not so clear. Just what was understood by being free has differed among political philosophers, or has not always been definitely clarified. Nevertheless, the ideas of the Ancients and Patristic doctrines influenced their followers and it is from the doctrines that evolved through following periods that we can discover how later thinkers came to conceive liberty.

The idea of freedom has always been closely associated with that of democracy, so just how the term is to be understood may well be grasped by examining the way in which the notion of democracy has developed in western Europe through history from Ancient times, through the Middle Ages and the Renaissance, up to the modern age. Historically democracy has been viewed as the political order that guaranteed freedom to the people from despotic and arbitrary enforcement by absolute rulers. So, in examining how the idea of democracy has evolved we shall also be discovering how the philosophers and political theorists conceived freedom. The tradition of democracy goes back to the Greeks whose word, meaning power to the people, it is, and the spirit of democracy is expressed by Thucydides in the funeral speech which he put into the mouth of Pericles:

Our constitution is named a democracy, because it is in the hands not of the few but of the many. But our laws secure equal justice for all in their private disputes, and our public opinion welcomes and honors talent in every branch of achievement, not for any sectional reason but on grounds of excellence alone. And as we give free play to all in our public life, so we carry the same spirit into our daily relations with one another. We have no black looks or angry words for our neighbor if he enjoys himself in his own way, and we abstain from the little acts of churlishness which, though they leave no mark, cause annoyance to whoso notes them. Open and friendly in all our private intercourse, in our public acts we keep strictly within the control of law. We acknowledge the restraint of reverence; we are obedient to whomsoever is set in authority, and to the laws, more especially to those which offer protection to the oppressed and those unwritten ordinances whose transgression brings admitted shame...

We are lovers of beauty without extravagance, and lovers of wisdom without unmanliness. Wealth to us is not mere material for vainglory but an opportunity for achievement; and poverty we think it no disgrace to acknowledge but a real degradation to make no effort to overcome. Our citizens attend both to public and private duties, and do not allow absorption in their own various affairs to interfere with their knowledge of the city's. We differ from other states in regarding the man who holds aloof from public life not as 'quiet' but as useless; we decide or debate, carefully and in person, all matters of policy, holding not that words and deeds go ill together, but that acts are foredoomed to failure when undertaken undiscussed. For we are noted for being at once most adventurous in action and most reflective beforehand.¹

In this manifesto Thucydides sets out both the general character of the citizens of a democratic state and the essential principles that democracy typically observes: protection of human rights, privilege and judgment based solely on merit, the rule of law the equality before the law of all citizens, equality of opportunity, the value and need for political discussion, tolerance of differing individual opinions, and willingness to differ without strife, with the ultimate recognition that the wisest decision is the outcome of rational argument. Pericles is referring to Athens, the most celebrated of the Greek democracies, but not all historians of Ancient Greece would agree that Thucydides' eulogy gives a true description of the Athenian democracy. Not only was Greek civilization tolerant of slavery, but other features of the political conduct of the Athenians appear to modern critics as improper in any true democracy. Possibly the most distinguished Athenian philosopher, Plato, although he certainly agreed with Thucydides' final contention that the most reliable conclusion issued from rational argument ("dialectic") and may have concurred with Thucydides' assessment in some other points, held a very different opinion of democracy, rating it as worse than every other form of government except tyranny. In a democracy, he observed, all are treated as equal whether they actually are so or are not; the prevailing obsession is money, and indiscriminate indulgence is tolerated in every sort of pleasure (whether necessary to life and health, or unnecessary and harmful). The characteristic features of democracy, he maintained, are immodesty, intemperance, insolence, imprudence, waste, and anarchy.[2]

Nevertheless, democracy became the preferred political form in the Ancient world until the first century A.D. The early Roman Republic continued the tradition for centuries, but it was thereafter submerged by the Roman Imperium and remained overwhelmed by its successor, the Holy Roman Empire. However, the Romans developed a system of law which recognized the rights of persons, even slaves, and principles universally applicable to all human beings, in the so-called Law of Nations. Hence there arose the notions of Natural Law, Natural Rights and a law of contract defining rights and duties.

These ideas were developed during the Middle Ages and resurfaced in the sixteenth and seventeenth centuries, in the works of such writers as George Buchanan, Duplessis Mornay, Althusius, John Milton, and John Locke, seeking to limit the despotic powers of Kingship. They first inspired the English rebellion against Charles I, and then the Glorious Revolution, which established democracy in Britain on a lasting basis, continuing the movement started centuries earlier by Simon de Montford.

A little over a hundred years later, after the philosophical doctrines had been further elaborated and modified by Montesquieu and Rousseau, they inspired the revolt of the American colonies against George III (proclaiming the slogan "No taxation without representation"), and then the French Revolution, which, in the nineteenth century, spread the ideas of liberty, equality, and fraternity across all Europe. These concepts were carried to the other continents by the colonial scramble of the European powers, and disseminated the western tradition of democracy which prevails today world-wide.

It will not come amiss to begin by reviewing the stages of this development in more detail. As already observed, it originates from Ancient times, and the more modern doctrines are rooted in that of a Law of Nature. The doctrine of Natural Law goes back to the Stoics and has even earlier origins. Its metaphysical significance is even greater today than it has been during its long history. I have explained why elsewhere,[3] but that is not our present concern. For the Stoics it was equivalent to the law of reason, an implication that it has always retained, and it was intended to serve as a standard for morals, law and politics. In the Middle Ages the Law of Nature was conceived as God's Law, of which there were three branches: the Divine Law supernaturally revealed to mankind for the redemption of the human race and the fulfillment of its eternal destiny; the Law of Reason, implanted by God for the attainment of mundane purposes: what followed from the pure Law of Nature as applying to the relationships between fallen human beings; and the Law of Nations, universal to all peoples (a concept obviously derivative from the Roman *jus gentium*). It was generally agreed that there was a Natural Law originating from a source transcending earthly power, before any political order existed, which was binding upon all men and all human institutions – a law universally obligatory, determining the rights of persons and regulating the relations between them; and the State itself, when it did come into being, owed its own authority and such rights as it claimed to this supreme *Lex Naturalis*. Even the highest earthly powers, Pope and Emperor, were subject to it, as was the entire community of mankind. Any positive law or act of any earthly ruler which contradicted the eternal and immutable principles of Natural Law was held to be null and void, and was obligatory upon nobody.

The Law of Nature was thus conceived as prior, both in authority and in time, to any social or political structure (and so to all positive law, or *jus civile*); and from it different theorists deduced opposite doctrines with respect to the supremacy of the monarch, whether in Church or Empire. Nevertheless, throughout the Middle Ages there was a strong tradition of popular sovereignty, the original right of the community being conceded even by those who contended for the monarch's (or the Pope's) supreme authority and his superiority to the positive law proceeded from the civil authority. This popular right was consequent to the divine establishment of a universal Church, which was held to include all mankind as God's children, and it was this *universitas fidelium* (community of the faithful), whose right and welfare was held to be prior to any authority set up by human action, whether by conquest or by agreement. The general conception entertained during the Middle Ages was of God as absolutely one, who created the world as a single organized cosmos (an idea owing much to the Ancients), and mankind as a single community, similarly ordered according to the principles of divine wisdom. From this it was not difficult to conclude that the will of the people took precedence over every other in temporal affairs, and many influential thinkers derived from it a theory of popular sovereignty.

A further support for the doctrine was the Teutonic conception of *Genossenschaft,* the idea of fellowship, combined with the notion of Corporation derived from Roman Law and enshrined in the Canonical rule. Hence arose the mediaeval conception of the right of Communities, and the view adopted of the relation between the community (or corporation) and its leader or head, which in time developed into a doctrine of the sovereignty of the people and of their relation to their ruler or rulers. These ideas were in harmony with the Patristic doctrine of a State of Nature in which the Law of God and the Law of Nature prevailed before the Fall of Man, from which it followed that only in consequence of that Fall was temporal rulership necessary. This was held to originate in a contract between the temporal ruler and the people who agreed to subject themselves to his authority. And, as all authority derived from the will of God, both the contract and the positive law which proceeded from the lordship it set up were subject to the Law of Nature. The power and authority of the ruler was then valid and his laws obligatory on his subjects only as long as he remained faithful to the terms of the contract, and if he violated them, or *ipso facto* the Law of Nature, he forfeited his right to rule. In such case, the people had a right of rebellion stemming from the Law of Nature itself.

The chief advocates of this doctrine were Marsilius of Padua and Nicolas of Cusa. Marsilius advocated a republican system in which power was divided between the civil community and the prince, the people being the legitimate source of legislation and the prince no more than their executive agent. The people's right to sovereignty, according to Marsilius, was inalienable, and was to be exercised either in a general assembly of the whole community, or through its elected representatives. The principle of election was generally recognized in the Middle Ages, even when the electors were not the common people, but, as in the case of the Emperor, the princes and prelates of the feudal fiefdoms, or in the case of the Pope, the College of Cardinals. The former were supposed to represent their subjects, and the latter the Community of the Faithful, the Church as a whole.

Nicolas of Cusa taught that all earthly power proceeded in the first instance from God, but the mundane agency of this power was the will of the Community of the Faithful (*universitas fidelium*) expressing God's will; and it was by the consent of the governed that any ruler had authority. It was only through this consent that the right of the ruler to govern could be regarded as having divine origin. Hence all jurisdiction and administration was derived from election and the transmission of power from the people to its representatives. Only in this way could a ruler be legitimately appointed, and, thus elected to public office, he became the bearer of the common will. Law-making was reserved to the Community, and the duty to obey depended upon the implied consent of the governed. The ruler was, like everybody else, subject to the law, and could act legitimately only within the mandate accorded to him by the people, by whom he could be deposed if he transgressed the limits set to his power by the Law of Nature.

As well as the ideas of popular sovereignty and contract, a conception of Natural Rights was also derived from that of Natural Law. In mediaeval theory secular power was always considered subject to the rules of Natural Law, even when it was held to be superior to positive law. Hence arose a distinction between two kinds of rights, those proceeding from positive law, which were simply concessions made by the secular authority, and those based on Natural Law, which were inalienable. Among the latter, rights and the duties correlative to them which flowed from contract were held to be rooted in Natural Law, so that a monarch could be bound by a contract originally made with his subjects. Further, in mediaeval doctrine, the Christian teaching prevailed that every individual had an eternal destiny, and so an absolute and ineluctable value; accordingly, the implication was universally presumed that, by Divine and Natural Law, every individual had inborn and inalienable rights. Here, then, we find the germ of the later doctrine of the Rights of Man prescribed by the Law of Nature.

The notion of the State was not characteristic of mediaeval thought, although the Ancient concept of the *polis*, especially as it is found in Aristotle's *Politics* was entertained by some writers, in particular Thomas Aquinas. Nevertheless, the monarchical authority attributed to the Emperor in secular affairs and to the Pope in spiritual, were progressively assimilated by the developing regimes becoming centralized in various European countries. Indeed, one mediaeval thinker, Marsilius of Padua, even went so far as to anticipate the claim that the Church was a state institution, and that the Ecclesiastical Community was identical with the Citizen Assembly whose jurisdiction was paramount in religious as well as in secular matters. With the advent of the Renaissance and subsequently the Reformation, the Ancient conception of the state was resuscitated and the secular Kingdoms claimed the supreme authority, which, in the Middle Ages, had been vested in the Community of the Faithful, and thence in Pope and Emperor. Political theory, from the 15th century onward proceeded to accommodate this development, and to speculate on the nature and source of sovereign power and its relation to the claims and rights of the individual. The solutions that it found to its problems were invariably based on the ideas which had been developing throughout the previous period, primarily that of Natural Law, and derivative therefrom those of Contract and Natural Rights.

The idea of a primordial law of Nature presupposes a State of Nature in which human beings lived before they formed organized societies with governmental arrangements. In this natural state, it was universally assumed, every person was free, independent and sovereign. Mutual relations between persons and conduct one towards another were governed by Natural Law, generally taken as identical with the Law of Reason. From this assumption different theorists derived different, and often opposing, doctrines of state sovereignty, its rights to obedience from its subjects, and the relations between the people and their rulers. But even in those which deduced that an inalienable right of absolute power must reside in the ruler (or rulers) there remained incipient germs of democratic principles.

Bodin, who declared that *majestas* was above all human laws and is illimitable and indivisible, argued in favour of a system of Estates which should meet regularly to apprise the King of their wishes and grievances, and give him advice. Hobbes deduced with unassailable logic that, human nature being what it is (aggressive, acquisitive and selfish), and in the State of Nature individuals being completely free of restraint, they would each seek their own advantage at the expense of all others. The result would be an intolerable condition of war of each against all, in which there could be no crafts or industry, no arts or society, a state in which everybody lived in constant fear and the danger of violent death. The only escape from this insufferable condition, as dictated by reason and its natural laws, was that every person should contract with every other to give up all their natural rights (i.e. powers) to one man (or body of men), who, said Hobbes, "would bear their Person", who would impose on them laws defining rights and duties to maintain the common safety of all, and in whom would reside an absolute right to their obedience.

Nevertheless, Hobbes realized that the will of the people could not altogether be disregarded. He preferred monarchy as the best form of government because he thought the personal interests of the monarch would be more completely identified with those of the people than would those of oligarchs or popular assemblies. He writes:

"Now in Monarchy, the private interest is the same with the publique. The riches, power, and honour of a Monarch arise only from the riches, strength and reputation of his Subjects. For no King can be rich, nor glorious, nor secure; whose subjects are either poore, or contemptible, or too weak through want, or dissention, to maintain a war against their enemies: Whereas in a Democracy, or Aristocracy, the publique prosperity conferres not so much to the private fortune of one that is corrupt, or ambitious, as doth many times a perfidious advice, a treacherous action, or a civil warre." (*Leviathan*, Part 2, Ch.XIX).

Moreover, Hobbes avers, a monarch can receive counsel and gather opinions from whom he will, those well versed in the matters with which he is concerned, be they of whatever rank. In other words, he may consult the wishes of his subjects. We may assume that he must do this constantly if those subjects are not to be "too weak through want, or dissention." And, as the monarch "bears the person" of each and every citizen, strictly speaking, the will of the people is expressed through his action.

For many other thinkers, however, the original freedom and sovereignty of the individual in the State of Nature constituted a basis for inalienable rights, which were maintained and protected in the Original Contract that established the civil state. George Buchanan, writing of the right of kingship among the Scots, assumes the existence of a state of nature prior to the civil condition, but draws attention to the lack of self-sufficiency suffered by persons in isolation. Such isolation is counteracted by the innate desire in all human beings for the company of their fellows; so the remedy is to form a society governed by law. He maintains that Kings are created and installed for the good of the people – not for their own interest which consists in the comfort and advantage they enjoy in ordered association. The function of the king is to preserve the good health of the society, as that of the physician is to preserve the health of the body, and it is the duty of the ruler to maintain justice, that is, "whatever is most favourable to the common concerns of men." Kingship is established by the people, he contends, for their own benefit and subject to laws which they have themselves promulgated; so that kings must promise, in taking the Oath of Office, to rule in accordance with those laws and to maintain them, in return for their subjects' obedience and loyalty. If the ruler breaks the law, he is as much subject to the courts as is any citizen, and if he abuses his power in a tyrannical manner, he may be removed from office and replaced, for he is subject to the authority of the people as a united body, as are all other magistrates.

One of the most influential treatises in the seventeenth century was *Vindiciae contra Tyrannos* (published over the pseudonym Junius Brutus, formerly thought to be by Languet, but now attributed to Duplessis Mornay). Here again an original state of nature is tacitly presumed and the civil condition comes into being as the result of a contract, first (establishing religion) between God and the people along with the prospective king, and then between the people and the king by which the former promise obedience and the latter just and equitable legislation. Much as was done during mediaeval times, the author distinguishes the office of the King (the Crown or Kingship) from his person, and asserts that officers of the state are representatives of the people, whose duty it is to keep the exercise of the King's power within legal bounds. The King's function is to adjudicate between individuals and to defend the territory of the state against incursion by neighboring peoples. The people, as one body, are superior to their ruler in that he is subject to the laws which he receives from them on his accession. The basis of government is thus the consent of the governed, in accordance with a contract which requires the ruler to act for the good of the populace and entitles the ruled to resist any attempt to impose tyranny.

Althusius sets forth a similar doctrine. The state of nature, for him, is already what he calls a symbiosis, for nobody could survive if abandoned in infancy, nor can the mature person acquire all the necessities of life unaided. But voluntary associations are based upon a tacit or overt contract between the members to co-operate for their mutual good. Every kind and degree of association, he thinks, rests upon a covenant prescribing the fundamental rules of the society. Accordingly, the supreme magistrate, the ruler of the state, is bound by the laws and provisions of the covenant which sets out the conditions of *imperium*: he submits to the obligation to administer the realm "according to laws prescribed by God, right reason, [clearly, the Law of Nature], and the body of the commonwealth." The right of sovereignty consequently belongs solely to the realm of the people as a whole, of which the supreme magistrate is no more than the steward.

The same conclusion based on virtually the same arguments as those of the *Vindiciae* is to be found in John Milton's pamphlet, *The Tenure of Kings and Magistrates*, which is little more than an endorsement of Duplessis' doctrine. In Milton's view, man is born free, in the image of God – his destiny is to rule and not to be ruled; but Adam's sin resulted in strife and dissension, which led men to contract to defend themselves against injury by agreeing to join forces and live according to prescribed laws, for which purpose it was necessary (as none could be trusted suffi-ciently to keep this undertaking) "to ordain some authority, that might restrain by force and punish what was violated against peace and com-mon right." This authority is derived from that originally vested in every person, which they then depute to one or a few to exercise as their commissioners, whose authority is curtailed by laws designed to limit their powers and restrain them should they become perverted or cor-rupt. Hence, kings and magistrates on their appointment are bound by oaths to administer justly and impartially, and parliaments are elected to keep them in check. So the power of kings is no more than what is en-trusted to them by the people, and if it is used otherwise than for the common good, the ruler may rightly be deposed and another installed.

The influence of John Locke in England and America was far-reaching during the later seventeenth and early eighteenth centuries. He provided, in the first instance, a theoretical justification for the English revolution of 1688. His teaching followed closely the ideas of his prede-cessors, especially Duplessis Mornay, but he gave a clearer and more detailed account of a State of Nature which contrasts strongly with what Hobbes had portrayed. For Locke the State of Nature was one of peace and tranquility governed by Natural Law, which every man defends for himself; but it involves the inconvenience that in cases of dispute each is judge in his own case, and there is no impartial judge to prevent conflict. To remedy this defect, men enter into compacts, first to resign to a pub-lic authority their rights of executing the Law of Nature each for him-self. This contract establishes a commonwealth. A second compact is then entered into by which the commonwealth delegates the exercise of its sovereign power to magistrates and legislative bodies, bringing into existence a constitution or government. The rights thus delegated, how-ever, are limited to what the common good requires:

> "…whoever has the legislative or supreme power of any commonwealth is bound to govern by established standing laws, promulgated and known to the people, and not by any extemporary decrees; by indifferent and upright judges who are to decide controversies by those laws; and to employ the force of the community at home only by the execution of such laws, or abroad to preserve or redress foreign injuries and to secure the community from inroads and invasion" (*Treatise of civil Government*, Ch. IX, Sect. 131).

Should the government violate these conditions by ignoring what is for the common good and by acting tyrannically, the obligation of the citi-zens to obey is rescinded, and the rulers may legitimately be replaced. Such a change of the legislature, as Locke calls it, does not dissolve the commonwealth, because the first stage of the Original Contract still holds and has not been broken; only the second stage has been violated, and that can be repaired by the people acting in concert as a commonwealth. The legislative set up by the people is considered superior, by Locke, to every other branch of government, but while at times he seems to identify it with the people who constitute it, at others he states explicitly that it is a merely fiduciary body limited to the common good and by the will and possible action of the people to remove and replace it. He writes:

> Though in a constituted commonwealth standing upon its own basis, and acting according to its own nature, that is, acting for the preservation of the community, there can be but one supreme power, which is the legislative, to which all the rest are and must be subordinate, yet the legislative being only a fiduciary power to act for certain ends, there remains still in the people a supreme power to remove or alter the legislative when they find the legislative act contrary to the trust reposed in them; for all power given with trust for the attaining of an end, being limited by that end, whenever that end is manifestly neglected or opposed, the trust must necessarily be forfeited, and the power devolve into the hands that gave it, who may place it anew where they shall think best for their safety and security. And thus the community perpetually retains a supreme power of saving themselves from the attempts and designs of anybody, even of their legislators whenever they shall be so foolish or so wicked as to lay and carry on designs against the liberties and properties of the subject... and thus the community may be said in this respect to be always the supreme power, but not as considered under any form of government, because this power of the people can never take place till the government be dissolved (Op. cit., Ch. xiii).

In the previous chapter, Locke has distinguished between the Legislative, the Executive and the Judicial powers of the state. While apparently regarding the last as an adjunct of the second, he subordinates the Executive to the Legislative and both to the popular will. Again, while he frequently refers to the people as "the community" he never regards them as anything but an aggregate of individuals, each with his [or her] innate natural rights, to be defended against any governmental power. Although Locke does not regard the various branches of government as mutually hostile, there is a strong suggestion, in the passages quoted, of a separation of powers. It is clear that he is anxious to limit the power of the Executive by that of the Legislature, and both by that of the people held in the background. But, apart from open insurrection, he does not make it clear how these mutual checks are to be exercised. Later thinkers, in particular Montesquieu, developed this suggestion into a full blown theory of division and balance of powers among government functions within the constitution. Montesquieu wrongly imagined that this division was inherent in the British constitution, which he greatly admired, overlooking the system of cabinet government being introduced by Walpole at that very time:

> When the legislative and executive powers are united in the same person, or in the same body of magistrates, there can be no liberty; for apprehensions may arise lest the same monarch or senate should enact tyrannical laws, to execute them in a tyrannical manner.

So he wrote in *L'Esprit des Lois*, (Book XI, Ch. vi). Each branch of government, he maintained should have the power of checking the other, when its actions went beyond legitimate bounds.

These doctrines had immense influence in the British American colonies. Locke had expressly declared (in Ch. xi) that the legislative "must not raise taxes on the property of the people without the consent of the people, given by themselves or their deputies." Here was the principle seized and acted upon by the Boston Tea-party and those they represented when the British government imposed taxation on the colonists to replenish its coffers after the costly wars against the French in Canada. Locke was invited to draft a constitution for Carolina; and the conception of division and balance of powers that he had suggested, that Montesquieu had systematically developed, and was expressly adopted ultimately in the Constitution of the United States.

All these theories and the practice based upon them, like Natural Law theories in general are individualistic. Even Althusius' recognition of the essential "symbiotic" character of human life fails to overcome this inherent individualism, for he presupposes as the basis of every type of association, whether private or public, a tacit or open contract between the individual members. This assumption, general among the thinkers we have been reviewing, is necessitated by the prior presupposition that in the State of Nature every person is sovereign and independent. Such tacitly presumed independent self-sufficiency was the background conception of freedom, and the preservation, or recovery, of natural rights, which was the persistent aspiration of theories insisting upon the limitation of the powers of the ruler and the ultimate sovereignty of the people. The ensuing conception of freedom was that of negative liberty entailing the right to be left alone, not to be interfered with, and the consequent freedom to do as one liked without hindrance or restraint, to acquire what property one could, and to live without fear of attack. These rights were held to be naturally innate and inalienable in every person. They were to be enjoyed, however, only in a manner that did not encroach upon the rights of others, and to ensure that this should be the case, and to settle any disputes which might arise between claimants, a system of control and regulation was seen to be necessary. To bring this about, then, was the aim of the Original Contract of each and every person with every other, to set up a government and to maintain a civil state. It was this notion of liberty that inspired the theorists and authors of the American Constitution, and which was expressed in the work of writers such as Thomas Paine. It is likewise the notion of liberty that underlies most of modern Liberal thought, and its constant accompaniment is the belief that government is a necessary evil, to be reduced to a minimum. The ultimate extreme of this attitude is that adopted by Thoreau in *Walden*. Nevertheless, among all these theories there prevails a tacit presupposition that the purpose of government is the preservation of the general welfare of the community (the people) and the prevention of arbitrary and oppressive acts by their rulers; so that the primary object of rulership is and should be a common good of which the popular will should be the ultimate criterion.

There were, however, other thinkers who realized that liberty involved more than freedom to do as one pleased, and that what so many conceived as liberty was simply license, the source of all conflict and disorder. If everybody enjoyed a right of this kind, then, no true freedom was possible, and the state of nature would be more truly as described by Hobbes than as assumed by Locke and his followers. The first philosopher to recognize this truth was Spinoza, who was strongly influenced by Hobbes and went some way in agreement with his doctrine; but he went far beyond both Hobbes and Locke in his conception of political freedom. He agreed with Hobbes that natural rights were the same as natural powers, but differed in maintaining that natural right was not forfeited by the individual in the civil state, because, Spinoza maintained, the Law of Nature was universally operative, so whatever one did in any circumstances one did by natural right. However, because human beings are "led more by blind desire than by reason", and are driven hither and yon by their passions, they fall to quarrelling and (as Hobbes had maintained) are by nature enemies. Their rights in the state of nature as generally conceived, Spinoza therefore concluded, would be nil.[4]

Spinoza had demonstrated in his *Ethics* that behavior prompted by passion is the result of external causes acting upon the human body, and is the product of *imaginatio* or inadequate thinking; but this can be raised to the level of *ratio*, which is adequate and true knowledge, consequent upon self-reflection, and caused only by one's own essence (which, he held was the intellect, or reason). This, therefore, is free action for in it the mind is the adequate cause of its own act. Accordingly, one has greatest power when guided by reason (adequate thinking), and that is genuine freedom. It follows that,

> ...a man in the state of nature is possessed of his own right, or free, only as long as he can protect himself from being subjugated by others; and his own unaided power is insufficient to protect him against all. Hence human natural right or freedom is a nonentity as long as it is an individual possession determined by individual power; it exists in imagination rather than in fact, since there is no certainty of making it good. Nor can it be disputed that the more cause for fear an individual has, the less power he has and in consequence the less right he has. Besides, it is hardly possible for men to maintain life and cultivate the mind without mutual help. I [Spinoza] therefore conclude that the right of nature peculiar to human beings can scarcely be conceived save when men hold rights as a body and thus have power to defend their possession of territories which they can inhabit and cultivate, to protect themselves, to repel all force, and to live in accordance with the common judgment of all. For....the more men there be that unite in this way, the more right they collectively possess... (*Tractatus Politicus*. Ch. ii, 15, Wernham's translation).

This corporate right, which is defined by the power of a people, Spinoza asserts, is generally called sovereignty. There can, then, be no question of limiting sovereign power in the interest of natural rights or individual freedom, because rights of any kind worth claiming can be enjoyed only through the exercise of the common power of a people, as Spinoza puts it, "led as if by one mind" and holding rights in common. For this, no contract is necessary, for, like everything else in the universe, human beings seek to preserve their own being, and pursue their best advantage, and nobody can doubt the superior advantage of living in accordance with law and the dictates of reason, which aim at and insure the true interests of each and every person alike (as Spinoza demonstrates in *Ethics* IV, Props. 35-37). All that is needed, therefore, is so to organize the agencies of government as to ensure a minimum of conflict, requiring efficient means of restraining passions and providing conditions in which the mind can be cultivated and life can be lived in a civilized and rational manner. Sovereignty thus resides in the joint will of the people operating through institutions of government devised by right reason, and individual rights are the better assured the more rational order is preserved. In fact, there are no rights except those recognized and protected by the commonalty:

> ...a citizen does nothing and possesses nothing by right unless he can defend it by the common decree of the commonwealth (*Tractatus Politicus*, Ch. III, 2).

For Spinoza, as for Hobbes, sovereignty is absolute but according to Spinoza it belongs to the community as a whole and not to any individual monarch or any body of representatives, who should exercise power only as prescribed by the constitution to fulfill a definite function, and may rule only with the consent of their subjects. This is not always done in the best way, even though it be done by right; but the more reason prevails, the better will be the organization of the state, which will vary as circumstances require. The essential point is that freedom is assured only in a rationally ordered state, and humankind is seen to be social by nature, even though not always, or generally, led by reason. For nobody can survive, much less "persist in his [or her] own being" without mutual co-operation between fellow human beings. Spinoza is well aware that political power is always and only derived from the common consent of the governed, for no one man, he asserts, has power enough to keep the multitude in subjection.

A hundred years elapsed between Spinoza's *Tractatus* and Rousseau's *Contract Social* in which the same recognition occurs, that political freedom is the fruit of social order and government. And that is to be strictly self-government. Rousseau uses the device of Contract, which (after toying with it in *Tractatus Theologico-Politicus*) Spinoza dropped altogether from the *Tractatus Politicus*; and even Rousseau's use of it, as of the State of Nature, was more in deference to tradition than from serious conviction. The contract for him was a surrender altogether of individual rights to the whole community from which all rights are "received back" to ensure that each person is "as free as before" (what he means, in effect, is genuinely free for the first time). The sovereign body now is the whole of the society and each member is subject to the General Will, which is strictly the will of every citizen, directed to the welfare of all the people in their mutual interdependence. The sovereignty of the General Will is (as with Locke) limited only to the common good, but otherwise (as with Hobbes) unlimited, inalienable and indivisible, and, Rousseau adds, infallible. It is always right, because it is always and only for the good of the whole, distinct from the particular will of the individual, which may diverge from it; and similarly distinct from the "will of all", which is no more than the fortuitous coincidence of the wills of individuals. We always will what is for our own good, says Rousseau, but we do not always recognize what that is. The people may be deceived, though it cannot be corrupted, and when the individual differences are allowed to cancel one another out, the general will remains. We shall see later, that there is more in this than meets the eye in Rousseau's text; the canceling out is really a complex process of criticism and discussion through which right reason eventually prevails.

Rousseau's work remained the inspiration not only of the French Revolution but also of later thinkers. Kant speaks of the original contract in much the same terms:

> the act the idea of which is presupposed in the state as a system of right, is the original contract, wherein the members of the people all and singular surrender their natural freedom in order to receive it again as members of a commonwealth – that is, the people regarded as a State. We should not then say that men in the State have sacrificed part of their innate natural freedom to secure an end; rather they surrender their wild lawless liberty altogether in order to find it again undiminished in a condition of dependence regulated by Law; for such dependence springs out of man's own legislative will (*Werke*, VII. p. 133. Hartenstein).

Man's legislative will, for Kant, is the source of all morality. It is the autonomous will of the rational being, the transcendental Ego, which determines itself, and imposes the categories of the understanding on its sensuous experience. This is the basis of the Good Will that wills itself and acts in accordance with the idea of law. As the root of moral obligation, it is also the source, Kant holds, of political obligation. This alone is what is free, and obedience to its injunction is perfect freedom.

Fichte likewise follows Rousseau, but the idea of contract, in his thought, becomes modified into that of an organic whole. As for Kant, so for Fichte, the original source of all action is, the Ego. Empirically, however, a self involves relations to other selves, and so to a society of selves; and law, or right, is the relation between selves as empirically posited by the Ego. The "contract" which establishes the state, is one to create a social whole in which "every part strives to conserve every part, because injury to any part may concern any part." Fichte, here, is developing ideas put forward by Kant in his *Critique of Teleological Judgment*, where he defines organism as a whole in which the parts are mutually ends and means. Fichte uses the notion of organism to describe the civic relation as a whole:

Just as, in the natural product, every part can be what it is only in this combination, and out of this combination simply would not be this (indeed outside all organic combination there would simply be nothing...): just so it is only in the combination of the State that man attains a definite position in the series of things, a point of rest in nature; and each attains this determinate position towards others, and towards Nature, only through the fact that he is in this determinate combination... In the organic body every part continually maintains the whole, and while it maintains it, is itself maintained thereby; just such is the citizen's relation to the State (*Werke*, III. p.207).

This line of reasoning led to the conclusion that political freedom is to be attained only in a rationally ordered state, constitutionally structured so as to give effect to the general will of the people in pursuit of a common interest, a form of government that protected individual and civil rights and provided the conditions of a good life for all.

Hegel, in the introduction to his *Philosophy of World History*, says that world history is the progress of the consciousness of freedom. Freedom he identified with the free self-reflective activity of thought: "He who rejects thought and speaks of freedom does not know what he is saying."[5] For Hegel, social organization is objective mind, and freedom is ensured by the rational organization of social functions through a constitution which sets every individual in a rational position within family, civil society, and government; the rights and duties relative to this social station are *Sittlichkeit*, the substance of ethical life, through which alone freedom can be achieved.

Thus, through the seventeenth and eighteenth centuries, three versions developed of a theory of sovereignty: the first, of which Hobbes is the typical representative, is the doctrine that the essential feature of political organization is a supreme authority imposing law and the final judge of its interpretation. This concept was taken up by jurists such as Sir William Blackstone and John Austin. Blackstone, in his *Commentaries on the Laws of England*, states of the various kinds of government,

However they began, or by whatever right they subsist, there is and must be in all of them a supreme, irresistible, absolute, uncontrolled authority, in which the *iura summi imperii*, or the right of sovereignty resides.[6]

Austin sums up the concept, in his *Province of Jurisprudence Determined*, in the definition:

If a *determinate* human superior, *not* in a habit of obedience to a like superior, receive *habitual* obedience from the *bulk* of a given society, that determinate superior is sovereign in that society, and that society (including the superior) is a society political and independent.[7]

Accordingly, this theory of sovereignty has been called appropriately the Juristic theory.

The second view of sovereignty insists on the rights of the subjects and the limitation of the governing authority to the common welfare. Its typical representative is Locke, and it may be called the Ethical theory. But the third conception of sovereignty is one that realizes the essential connection of the other two, which are seen to be necessary aspects of any successful political organization. Spinoza and Rousseau expounded this idea of political authority and it has been called the philosophical theory, the development of which will be the subject of our next chapter.

Certainly freedom is the central theme of the history of modern political philosophy. Those who affirmed the absolute power of the sovereign stressed the futility of permitting unrestricted individual freedom and the need, if security of life and property were to be ensured, of an unassailable authority to enforce law. Those who were concerned to prevent and resist despotism insisted on the natural rights of the individual as an unchallengeable limit to the powers of the ruler. But, in the end, philosophers came to see that actual freedom was attainable only in a well organized society regulated by law enforced by a government which ruled by popular consent. Theories appealing to Natural Law, assuming a pre-civil State of Nature, tended, as we have seen, to be individualistic – assuming that the natural man was a self-sufficient, independent, creature, seeking his own advantage in competition with all others. But after Rousseau, the philosophers recognized the essentially social nature of humanity and the consequent necessity of rationally structured social order to secure domestic peace and justice within the community. Law must indeed be enforceable, and there must be a supreme authority to legislate, interpret and administer sovereign enactments; but this supreme authority should and can only draw its power from the concerted and unified will of the people who submit to it, and its legitimacy from its service of the common good.

Thus emerged a theory of self-government, of popular sovereignty issuing in the institution of constitutional democracy. Democracy is thus seen to be the sovereignty of the people, absolute as maintaining the Rule of Law, but exercising the supreme power only on condition that it serves the common good of the whole community. Sovereignty, as Spinoza has told us, is the whole popular body "acting as with one mind"; and the sole justification of its supremacy and authority is that it aims at attaining the common safety and welfare of the community as a whole. In such a community freedom is not simply licence, it is not just the right to be left alone – to be unrestricted in pursuing one's personal aims. It is the security of life in a society of interacting and co-operating citizens, the mutual intercourse of whom generates a tradition of common thought and will aiming at a common good.

NOTES

---

[1] Thucydides, *The Peloponnesian War*, Edited in translation by Sir R.W. Livingstone, (Oxford, Oxford University Press, 1943), Bk.II, pp. 37,40

[2] Cf. Plato, *The Republic*, pp. 558c-561c.

[3] Cf. *Cosmos and Theos* (Atlantic Highlands, NJ, Humanities Press, 1991), pp. 33-35.

[4] Cf. *Tractatus Politicus*, Ch.II, pp. 15.

[5] My translation. Cf. *Vorlesungen uber die Geschichte der Philosophie*, III (Theorie Ausgabe, Frankfurt-am-Main, Suhrkamp, 1978), Band 20, p.308; Hegel's *Lectures on the History of Philosophy*, Translated by E.S.Haldane and F.H. Simson (London, Routledge and Kegan Paul, 1968), Vol. III, p. 402.

[6] *Commentaries*, vol. I, p. 49.

[7] Op. cit., pt. I, ¶ i, lect. 6.

2. More Recent Theories of Democracy

The traditional tendency to interpret liberty individualistically as simple absence of restraint, persisted into the nineteenth century, having been re-emphasized by Bentham, who, considered law to be inevitably opposed to freedom, which he identified with the enjoyment of pleasure. Such individual enjoyment could only be reduced by the necessary restraints imposed by the law, the aim of which, he held, was the maximization of pleasure of the greatest number, a goal which could be reached, where means were limited and persons were in competition to acquire them, only if individual pleasures were curtailed in the interests of others' enjoyment. In succession to him (and James Mill), John Stuart Mill, consequently maintained that no activity could legitimately be restricted by law unless it encroached upon the liberty of others, and all purely self-regarding action should be immune from government interference. Liberty is thus identified with idiosyncrasy and eccentricity rather than with a well ordered and harmonious life in society, and government becomes inveterately opposed to freedom. The effect was to see government as a necessary evil to be limited strictly to the prevention of the encroachment by others on the unrestrained liberty of the individual. This was the view adopted by Herbert Spencer in his work, *Man versus the State*, where he represents the influence of society and the State as purely negative, inevitably infringing on rights, which (he believed) inhered solely in individuals and could never be conferred by law. An extreme version of this position was set out still later by J. Seeley in his *Introduction to Political Science*, where he writes: "Perfect liberty is equivalent to total absence of government" (see p.119).

Of course, such "perfect" liberty was recognized to be unattainable, because of the inevitable encroachment by other individuals upon the free exercise of will by each. Hence the need for government and regulation, but these were no better than unavoidable restrictions. Not only do such views fail to recognize the essentially social nature of human beings, but they set government and freedom in irreconcilable opposition, which, in the nature of the case, renders freedom unattainable and government inexorably suspect as incipient tyranny.

Under the strong influence of Hegel the British Idealists opposed this trend, following the guiding thread offered by Rousseau and the course it prompted in the thinking of Kant and Fichte. They were strongly critical of the Utilitarians and of Spencer, seeking in contrast to evolve a theory of self-government which was essentially democratic and represented political obligation as a moral duty owed to a state that genuinely represented the true and legitimate will of the people. Ideally this "General Will" embodied the moral ideal and thus represented the conscience of the individual, so that obedience to the moral law and obedience to the law of the land converged, at least in principle, the latter being nothing other than the self-determination of the free will of the individual citizen in obedience to a self-imposed law. This was the case, however, only for democratic regimes in which the law expressed the popular will and in the ideal case *vox populi* coincided with *vox Dei*.

For T.H. Green, the human person is a self-conscious subject embodied in a natural organism. As self-conscious and conscious of its own sensations and natural inclinations it is transcendent (in the Kantian sense that it is the precondition of the perception of its phenomenal object) and therefore cannot be identified with the flow of its naturally conditioned consciousness, with any sequence of its phenomena or sensations, or with any of its natural inclinations. The human good, in consequence, is not to be found in the satisfaction of any particular natural desire, nor any mere sequence of such satisfactions, but is the realization of an ideal of the self which will satisfy it as good for its own sake. As personality is essentially a social product, the satisfaction of the self necessarily includes that of other selves, who as rational self-conscious persons seek the same end. The good is thus a common good, identical for all and at once social as well as personal.

Moreover, as the self-conscious subject is transcendent and necessarily distinct from all its sequential conscious states, it cannot be a temporal entity. The knowledge of the world that it acquires through the medium of its consciousness is relational: the ordered system of interrelated objects, involving awareness of the terms as related. The conscious sub-ject cannot therefore be identified with any one, or any collection, of these terms but must be eternal. Because of the limitations imposed on consciousness by the natural conditions of organic life, the knowledge of the world so acquired is always partial and deficient, yet as an ordered system it is such as to imply and require, for its attain-ment, the complete and total reality, in principle infinite – i.e., the mind of God. T.H. Green therefore concludes that the rational self is the di-vine spiritual principle operating within a finite living organism, which it uses as an instrument for the acquisition by the finite self of knowledge and for the attainment of the common good. To seek the fulfillment of the rational self in the pursuit of the common good is, therefore, no less than the service of God, which is perfect freedom; and in so far as a so-ciety recognizes and acknowledges this, *vox populi* is indeed *vox Dei*.

Here too we have the key to freedom: a rational will is by definition free, because it is the activity of the transcendental ego, so its action cannot be the result of any phenomenal cause but is determined only by itself. Its ultimate object is self-realization, which can be fully satisfied only by the attainment of the ideal – the common good. The content of the will, however, is supplied by natural wants and appetites, with the fulfillment of which, rightly or wrongly, one identifies the satisfaction of self. Pursuit of particular ends may conflict both one with another and with those of other persons' desires, and such conflicts obstruct the at-tainment of a common good. So the pursuit of particular desires may in fact, although the choice be freely made, actually limit freedom as de-fined by self-realization. Freedom, in consequence, is not license to do as one pleases without interference, but is the ordering of one's desires and activities so as willingly to conform to the requirements of the common good. It is for this reason that the service of God is perfect freedom. Green's conception of sovereignty is a combination and reconciliation of those put forward by Rousseau, on the one hand, and John Austin,[1] on the other.

Green contends that where there is such a determinate superior as Austin presumes, the bulk of the society will render habitual obedience only if and because they regard the superior as embodying what may properly be called the general will, and in the conviction that the law imposed by the superior conduces to their common interest. The obligation to obey is not the product of mere compulsion, but derives from the same source as moral obligation. That government depends on the consent of the governed, he says, is a confused way of stating the truth, that the institutions by which man is moralized, by which he comes to do what he sees that he must, as distinct from what he would like, express a conception of a common good; that through them that conception takes form and reality; and it is in turn through its presence in the individual that they have a constraining power over him, a power that is not that of mere fear, still less a physical compulsion, but which leads him to do what he is not inclined to because there is a law that he should."[2]

The source of moral obligation is the recognition that certain regulations governing conduct are necessary to the attainment of a common good, and that of political obligation is the same: submission to law is conditional upon the recognition that it protects those rights of the individual necessary to ensure a common good. Compulsion is necessary only as a reminder of their obligations to those led by natural inclination to ignore and resist these regulations; it is not the source of the obligation.

It follows that government, in principle, must express the will of the people, however best evidenced, which may not always be through the vote in an assembly of representatives, or even directly through the vote of the entire body of citizens, for their judgment may be mistaken in any particular case; but the basic assumption is, and must be, that when everybody votes for what he or she genuinely believes is for the good of the whole community, the general will is given effect.

The doctrine of the general will is further elaborated by Bernard Bosanquet to whose exposition we may turn next. Bosanquet develops Rousseau's doctrine in the light of Hegel's advances, and he gives a singularly enlightening analysis of the way in which the general will is generated and made effective. Despite his endeavor to see society as a corporate body, Rousseau is still so far influenced by the individualism of the Natural Law theories as to regard the state as a collection of citizens, whose general will can only be ascertained from a vote of the assembly of the entire body. He neglects, or even discounts, prior discussion. He sees that this involves the danger that individuals voting in their own interests will give rise to what he calls "the will of all" in contrast to the general will, and he never fully succeeds in solving the problem of how to get over this difficulty. Hegel, in contrast, recognizes the essentially social character of the individual, who, through inevitable membership first of a family and then of an ascending range of social organizations, from professional guilds to the state, thinks from the first in terms of common ends. It is within the institutions of this social order, what Hegel calls *Sittlichkeit*, that the general will comes into being.

Taking his cue from Hegel, Bosanquet insists that there is a common consciousness among the members of every society, in which the members cooperate for a common purpose, a consciousness operative only in individual minds, yet including the views of all the others seen in each case from a particular point of view. This common consciousness is for the most part unrecognized by the persons in whom it is active; in general it is traditional and customary. But when individual wills tend towards self-centered ends they are modified by intercommunication and discussion with other, sometimes initially conflicting, views of other members of the society – an intercommunication and discussion that involves mutual criticism.

Within the social order the best interest of every member coincides with the common interest of the whole group, for it is only through the cooperation of all the members that any interest can be reliably assured. The common good is, therefore, what will really satisfy every member. Individuals, however, are liable to be short-sighted and to see only their own particular immediate advantage. This is what Bosanquet calls the actual will of the person so disposed. But what is actually willed in this manner is not what will really, in the long run, satisfy the person so willing, because it is liable to be frustrated by the opposition of those on whose assistance and co-operation it depends. The individual's real will, therefore, is what is in the common interest of the whole society. The actual will, because it comes into conflict with other individual wills directed similarly at their own immediate advantage, is liable to be frustrated in practice and so tends to be modified. The resolution of such conflicts occurs through criticism of actual wills in the course of discussion, which (as we shall see later) takes a variety of forms in a democratic society, and which corrects and modifies the actual wills of the individual citizens in the direction of their common interest, generating their general will.

The process is very complex and varied. It begins in the family, whose common interest exercises a powerful influence on the thinking of its individual members. It continues in the mutually complementary functions and division of labour in the economic system, in social and political organizations, cooperative societies, trade unions, corporations, political parties, and the like. In all these social institutions the individual's actual will is progressively modified and adjusted to harmonize with the wills of others, until finally in the deliberations of a legislative assembly a general will of the whole community emerges. This, through the legislature, becomes the sovereign will of the democratic state as a whole.

Bosanquet identifies the state with the entire gamut of social activities and functions encompassed by the community, including what others call civil society and seek to distinguish from the state, which they conceive as confined to the institutions of government. These institutions, although of special importance, are not what Bosanquet considers to be the state, as such, but are only specific institutions with specific governmental functions within the state, just as are other institutions with other specific functions. In this respect, Bosanquet follows Hegel, for whom the state as a whole is the union of the family, the civil society (*bürgerliche Gesellschaft*), and the government, which, as the authority that regulates their activities and adjudicates and settles disputes within civil society in general, is the reconciliation of the contrast between them.

Many thinkers who oppose civil society to the state continue the tradition of individualistic theories, which see law and regulation as a limitation on freedom rather than the means of its realization through the protection of legitimate rights. The individualist tradition regards rights as natural and prior to the civil condition, a position rejected by Green and Bosanquet, for whom rights exist only within ordered societies whose members recognize one another as equals, as ends in themselves. It is from this mutual recognition alone that rights and duties derive, and it is only from this that one can decide what rights ought to be recognized, which (in any particular society) may not be. Apart from mutual recognition of persons there can be no prior "natural" rights attaching to individuals as such, as if they could exist independently of society and mutual recognition. The law does not always, or ever, recognize and protect all the rights which ought to be admitted; and what have been called "natural rights" (so T.H. Green asserts) are simply those which are morally requisite in consequence of the social recognition of persons as ends in themselves. They cannot be anterior to social order. For Bosanquet, rights are incident upon social function. They are those liberties that must be guaranteed by the law if persons are to be able to perform their social functions as well as possible and to develop their personalities to their full capacity.

The democratic state, according to the thinkers we have been reviewing, is one in which the whole community participates, through its civil and administrative institutions, in a process of intercommunication, commerce and discussion, which generates a general will that, because it represents the common good of the social whole, is supreme and thus exercises sovereign authority invested in the institutions of government.

These theories, especially Bosanquet's conception of the real will, have been subjected to criticism, much of it based on misunderstanding.[3] But, for our present purpose, we need not examine such criticisms in detail, as they are directed, for the most part, against special philosophical concepts and not against the general notion of democracy as popular sovereignty. L.T. Hobhouse is Bosanquet's most vocal critic. He objects to the conception of a "real" will as distinct from an "actual" will. Only the actual will, in his opinion, is real, and what Bosanquet calls the real will of the citizen is not real at all, but at best only an ideal. It has to be observed, however, that what one wills is always ideal. I will what I conceive to be a better state of affairs and of myself than what actually exists. Thus, what Bosanquet calls "actual" will and what he calls "real" will are both ideal; but the first is a misconception of what is really intended, an immature and undeveloped form of what it becomes in the course of practical implementation and social criticism. For Bosanquet, who thinks teleologically, what anything is really is what it is when fully developed.

Bosanquet has also been criticized for identifying the general will with the state and thus the state with the moral ideal. The state in this way is held by the critics to become immune from criticism and reform. But this is a misconception; Bosanquet insists that the general will (and so the state) is the product of continual and on-going criticism, and the need for reform and improvement is a constant requirement.

Even writers like R.M. MacIver, who is more concerned with the practical exigencies of government than with philosophical theory, and who treats the state as only one association among many within the national community, accepts the idea of the general will, not as conceived by Rousseau as the legislating agency, but as a basic and background will to maintain the community. He regards the ultimate sovereign as the will of the people, which he does not identify with the general will, but sees as what wins through to constitute a government in the hurly burly of political conflict between parties. For him, the general will unites winners and losers:

> It is the will of membership, of communion, the will that identifies a citizen with all that he divines of the meaning and service, tradition and promise, of the state... It is the deeper sea of devotion that knows nothing of the waves that rock the surface of politics.[4]

In his book, *The Modern Democratic State*, A.D. Lindsay admits the significant contribution made by Bosanquet, but he tends to brush aside, as if rejecting, the Hegelian elements in Bosanquet's theory. Yet Lindsay himself adopts the essential feature of Hegel's doctrine that in the modern state the constitution has come to assume the status of the sovereign. Hegel insists that the constitution represents the way in which the social whole is organized, and it is this organization that is the paramount determinant of the life of the citizens. Lindsay maintains that the rule of law must prevail. The question, however, arises who makes, administers, and interprets the law and that is determined by the constitution which is thus the final authority. Lindsay also accepts the idea of the general will, which he identifies as the spirit of the common life of the community; but he contends that Rousseau and his followers (especially Green and Bosanquet), in their endeavor to refute the doctrine that liberty means the absence of government, go too far and prove too much when they argue that the general will is the individual's real will, and that in obeying the law the citizen obeys only him or her self (his or her own best will), so that liberty and obedience coincide. This position, he maintains, fails because its proponents provide no criterion by which to distinguish the general will from the will of all.[5]

It should be evident, however, that Bosanquet distinguishes the general will from particular actual wills (or the fortuitous coincidence of particular wills) by the fact that the former is the product of social criticism and debate, which corrects the casual wills of individual persons by forcing them to modify what they pursue when they are constrained to act in concert to produce a common policy that is concordant with the best judgment that the community can provide. And Lindsay repeatedly asserts that the primary characteristic of democracy is discussion. This, then, he ought to recognize, provides the critical hall-mark for distinguishing when the commands of the government are an expression of the general will and when they are not: they are when they conform to the approved result of social discussion and criticism. More will be said below about the constitutional process of political discussion by which the expression of the general will through the acts of the government is ensured.

Lindsay alleges that Bosanquet's arguments are compatible with Hitler's claims – in effect, that they are compatible with totalitarianism. But this is surely a misrepresentation, for Bosanquet insists on the free interaction of civil associations and he limits state action strictly to that of hindering hindrances to the good life.[6] Lindsay likewise contends that

democratic government must be restricted to maintaining the minimum conditions necessary for the general welfare, and to the protection
of rights that ensure free activity by voluntary associations – a view that
more or less concurs with Bosanquet's.

On the whole then, even the critics embrace the same basic conception of democracy as government by popular consent, in which the
popular will is supreme, as generated through a process of social discussion and deliberation organized within a legally constituted framework
of legislative and administrative institutions.

Bosanquet had demonstrated how the actual wills of the citizens in
a democracy, through criticism, opposition, discussion and compromise
(as well as correction through practical experience) become converted
into the general will of the community, which is what they all really
want, if they could but know it. Ernest Barker has explained how this
process is organized and institutionalized as the essential democratic process.[7] Democracy, he maintains, is government by and through
discussion, which is a continuous process with definite and coordinated
stages, distinct yet intrinsically connected and mutually dependent.
Barker's description of a democratic society is worth quoting. He writes:

> So far as the society of selves exists by formal rule, it exists as a scheme
> for the adjustment of relations... So far as society exists by dynamic proc-
> ess, it exists for and by mutual interchange of conceptions and convictions
> about the good to be attained in human life and the methods of its attain-
> ment. It thus exists for and by a system of social discussion, under which
> each is free to give and receive, and all can freely join in determining the
> content or substance of social thought – the good to be sought, and the
> way of life in which it issues. Now such discussion is also... the essence of
> democracy.[8]

Discussion occurs throughout a democratic society, in both civil and
political spheres; but in the civil sphere, within and among voluntary associations, it is diffuse and uncoordinated, although not unimportant
for, or unconnected with, political discussion. The latter, however, is an
organized process going through definite and specific stages. The first
stage occurs in the political party, which is itself a social as well as a political association. Through discussion among its members it evolves a
program and a policy and selects persons to represent it and to present
its policy to the electorate. The second stage is discussion within the
electorate, between parties and in the press, as well as between individuals at political meetings. The result of this stage is the election of members of parliament respectively supporting the different parties, to initi-

ate the third, distinct and different level of discussion – parliamentary debate – the object of which is to enact legislation. The election also decides which party is in the majority and will thus have the confidence of Parliament, enabling it to form a government. The legislation presented to parliament is initiated by the cabinet, in which the fourth stage of the process of political discussion is conducted, both among its members and between it, as the government, and the shadow-cabinet set up by the opposition. Discussion also occurs between parliament and the cabinet (for instance, in Prime Minister's question time), determining that each retains the confidence of the other.

Each of these stages is complementary to the others. They successively continue the necessary and typically democratic process, and although they are distinctive and different each from the next they are mutually interdependent and do not function successfully unless they keep in mutual contact. The party, to be effective and to succeed in its quest for power, must woo the electorate, and the electorate must monitor the conduct of the party both before and after it is elected, whether it is in power or in opposition (at the present time this process is recorded in public opinion polls). Parliament cannot dissociate itself from the electorate, and the cabinet remains responsible both to the electorate and to parliament. Yet the discussion at each stage is on a different level and has a different purpose, all contributing indispensable phases to the ultimate process of government.

A further and separate stage of discussion occurs through the judicial system, in the courts, where the pros and cons of every disputed case are set out and examined. Discussion occurs between the advocates of the plaintiff and the defendant, between each of these and the witnesses (in cross-questioning), between judge and advocates, when occasion arises, and, in the judge's summing up, between judge and jury. There is also discussion among the members of the jury in their attempt to reach a decision; so that the final verdict is the result of the complex discussion constituting the conduct of the case. For the most part, judges pronounce their judgments in accordance with existing law, but when the interpretation of the law is in doubt, the judge's decision is itself a form of law-making.

In these various ways, in a democracy, discussion is the process of government, in the making of laws, in their administration, and in their application to specific cases. It is also the process by which the persons of the government are elected, and its policies are decided. It is the process of generation of the general will of the people and the way in which it is made effective. Government so conducted is, in Barker's words,

> ...a government depending on mutual interchange of ideas, on mutual criticism of the ideas interchanged, and on the common and agreed choice of the idea which emerges triumphant from the ordeal of interchange and criticism. A government depending on such a process can enlist in itself and its own operation the self of every member. It will be self-government: it will square with, and be based upon, the development of personality and individuality in every self. It will be government by the people not as a mass, or as a majority, but as a society of living selves. In that sense it will be a democracy.[9]

The presupposed conditions of such discussion are, on the one hand, a common social tradition and a common interest in major underlying issues. On the other hand, and even more important, there must be a universal agreement to differ, in the sense that different opinions are respected, a willingness in consequence to compromise, and an acknowledgement that the resulting majority view must prevail as the emergent opinion of the whole body. Barker insists that the issue is not the rule of the majority as a form of dictatorship. It is not the overruling or suppression of the minority. The essence of discussion is that each opposing view influences the other; the proponents of each party must be open to conviction by argument and will, in consequence, modify its own position in the light of the discussion. The final majority view then contains elements of the minority opinion, and the minority position has been modified in the direction of that to which it has been opposed. The final outcome, therefore, is much nearer to a consensus than just an overriding and annihilating majority decision.

These presupposed conditions are of the utmost importance because, unless they obtain, there can be no assurance of the eventual emergence of a general will. For democracy to be genuine and to succeed they must be observed by every party, throughout the electorate, and they must be the constant and universal assumption behind parliamentary debate. If the party line is mere dogma, and its proponents are not open to persuasion, there is no possibility of genuine discussion. If the electorate splits into irreconcilable factions, the result can only be strife and no rational discussion is possible. If party discipline in the House is so rigid that voting reflects only the instruction of the whips, genuine interchange of views is undermined, and the dictatorship of the majority becomes a reality. The presupposition of the democratic process is that persons are rational and that argument between different opinions aims at discovering the truth and determining the common good. If these assumptions fail, government ceases to be self-government, interchange of opinions degenerates into irreconcilable conflict and rulership becomes imposition by the force of one faction upon the rest. But even short of this dire result, the practice of professed democracies can deteriorate and become corrupted in ways that are to be examined in later chapters of this book.

Finally all this may be summed up in the conclusion that genuine democracy is the sovereignty of the people, who by a system of discussion and criticism, in civil society and in the institutions of government, of differing and conflicting opinions and interests arrive as closely as practicable to the general will of the populace – the will to realize the well-being of the nation and guarantee its security.

This conception of democracy is genuinely idealistic, and even its advocates admit that in actual practice it may not be realized completely, but it stands as an ideal that genuine democrats ought to recognize and at which they should sincerely aim. Whether in the twenty-first century such recognition and adoption of the conceived tradition still prevails in any degree, or whether it has been obscured by contemporary world conditions and forgotten, is what we shall seek to consider in what follows.

The background inspiration of these theories, especially Bosanquet's, being Hegel's *Rechtsphilosophie*, something should be added in reference to subsequent criticisms of Hegel and those whom he influenced, some of which (e.g., that of Sir Karl Popper in *The Open Society and its Enemies*) are so ill supported and unscholarly as hardly to deserve serious refutation. They are simply examples of gross misunderstanding supported by misquotation or quotation out of context. Isaiah Berlin, in his *Essays on Liberty*, was to a considerable extent responsible for the reaction against the Idealist position, through his critique (albeit qualified) of its presumed possible influence on contemporary political developments. Like some others (e.g., E.F. Carritt) he argues that the contentions of such thinkers as Green and Bosanquet and especially of Hegel could be used to justify Fascism, Nazism and dictatorship in general, a submission which any careful examination of the relevant texts is bound to dispel.

Hegel has often been represented as the father of Prussianism, the eulogist of war, and the advocate of totalitarianism. His *Rechtsphilosophie* has been decried as truckling to the Prussian authorities. That Hegel deserves no such accusations has been decisively and convincingly demon-

strated by Sir Malcolm Knox, who has pointed to passages in his writing
and circumstances at the time of his appointment to the Chair of Philosophy in Berlin which clearly exonerate him from these charges. The
main lines of his political theory were laid down long before he was appointed to the Berlin Chair and cannot, if only for that reason, have
been concocted simply to please the Berlin authorities. Knox has drawn
attention to Hegel's early enthusiasm for the principles inspiring the
French Revolution and his regular celebration of its anniversary (despite
his criticism of the nature and practice of the Terror). Recent publication
of transcripts of Hegel's lectures on *Naturrecht und Rechtsphilosophie*
have also clearly shown (as the editors have pointed out) that such accusations are entirely misconceived and misplaced:

> The key concept of Hegel's Philosophy of Right is freedom and his aim is
> to demonstrate how political organization is the necessary means of mak-
> ing freedom actual. He does so, not by attempting to construct an ideal
> state, nor is he seeking to describe the form of any state existing in his day;
> he is investigating the essential features of social order that are characteris-
> tic of the modern state as such. He explicitly says that he is not concerned
> with particular historical states, any or all of which may be defective, or
> corrupt in some way or another, but that he is seeking to expound the es-
> sential philosophical nature of a state. This he says will be true of all [mod-
> ern] states however defective, just as some men are criminals, or imbeciles,
> but are nevertheless men. Accordingly, we may assume that, had there
> been in Hegel's day a fascist regime, he would have regarded it merely as a
> corrupt version of what he was expounding. [a]

---

[a] T.M. Knox, "Hegel and Prussianism", *Philosophy*, Vol. XV, No.57, 1940,
pp. 51-63. Cf. also, my review of the recently published three volumes of
Hegel's Lectures on *Naturrecht* and *Die Philosophie des Rechts* in *The Journal of
the History of Philosophy*, Vol 25, No.2, 1987, Hegel *Philosophie des Rechts*,
Herausgegeben von Dietrich Henrich; G.W.F. Hegel: *Die Philosophie des
Rechts*, Herausgegeben von Karl-Heinz Ilting; G.W.F.Hegel *Vorlesungen:
Ausgewählte Nachschriften und Manuskripten*, Herausgegeben von C. Becker, B.
Bonsiepen (et al.), and "Hegel's Theory of Sovereignty, International Rela-
tions and War" in *Hegel's Social and Political Thought*, Ed. Donald P. Verene
(Atlantic Highlands NJ, Humanities Press; Sussex, England, Harvester
Press, 1980). See also F. Neuhouser, *Foundations of Hegel's Social Theory*, es-
pecially pp. 130 and 308n14 where he notes that (a) an essential feature of
Hegel's conception of the purpose of the social whole is that it provide the
conditions of individual freedom, and (b) that this appears explicitly only in
the 1820 version of the *Rechtsphilosophie*. This is clear evidence that the pub-

Like Aristotle, he believed that human beings are rational and self-conscious, capable of critically reflecting upon their own actions, both intellectual and practical. From birth they are dependent on their parents and subsequently upon their fellows. In consequence, they are social animals and their social institutions are basically, in varying degrees, rational. The central question he is addressing is: By what criterion do we judge the rationality, the adequacy and efficiency, of those institutions? And the answer he gives is: The degree to which they foster freedom and render it actual. It is, therefore, not credible that he would have approved of totalitarian dictatorship.

What Hegel says of freedom in the *Rechtsphilosophie* must be understood in the light of what he has said about the freedom of the will and individual personal freedom in the *Phenomenologie* and the section on Subjective Mind in the *Geistesphilosophie*, where he makes plain that personal freedom is consequent upon freedom of the will but that it is no better than an abstract idea unless and until it can be actualized in practice – until it is objectified. Freedom proper, therefore, is the free activity of practical reason. The persistent thesis of the whole system of Hegel's philosophy is that the essential capacity of humanity is to be a self-conscious rational person, but nobody can realize this capacity except within a rationally ordered society the institutions of which have progressively developed in the course of history. Hence personal freedom and social (political) freedom are two sides of the same coin.

The historical development of political forms and institutions are thus the evolution of the conditions of freedom. As we noted at the end of the last chapter, Hegel maintained that "world history is nothing but the development of the concept of freedom." Orientals, he considered, were not free because they did not realize that man, as conscious spirit, is free; they only knew that one was free – the despot. The Greeks and Romans, who countenanced slavery, knew only that some were free. But contemporary Europeans, under the influence of Christianity, recognize that all human beings are free. And their freedom is at once personal (subjective) and, if it is actual, social (objective). It is essentially self-conscious: "....whoever neglects thought and speaks of freedom does not know what he is saying" (*Lectures on the History of Philosophy*, Ch. II, C4).

---

lication of the *Grundlinien* was no attempt to truckle to the Berlin authorities.

Hegel's conception of freedom is complex. To explain it in full would require a virtual treatise. All we need to know, however, in order to acknowledge that he could not have approved of totalitarian dictatorship, is the essential aspects of his position. Freedom, for Hegel is not license, nor is it merely exemption from interference; it is self-determination – determination by no external things or causes, but solely by itself. That is why freedom is a complex concept, for determination (as Spinoza had told us, and as Hegel concurs) involves negation. What determines anything is what limits it – what it is not. Hegel insists, however, that speculative reason (in contrast to mere understanding) negates the negation, seeing that what determines anything defines it. A conscious being, moreover, being aware of its own limitations, of what determines it and obstructs its action, makes its other its own, primarily in knowledge, and then in practice, by striving to overcome the opposition and alter the external conditions to conform to what it desires and approves. Thus self and other unite and are (in more ways than one – subjectively in knowledge and objectively in practice) identical. In striving to modify its other to conform to what it will accept and approve, the self determines both other and itself – overcomes its limitations and negates its negation. As Hegel constantly asserts, the self "finds itself at home in its other."

Human freedom is still further complex, involving not only freedom of the will (an essential feature of self-consciousness), but freedom to judge and choose what is good. To be self-determined the will must not be determined by external factors among which are the instinctive urges and appetites of a living being stimulated by external causes. The conscious mind, however, distinguishes itself from its own feelings and instinctive promptings and is able to choose between them, selecting by its own choice which of them it will follow. This, Hegel calls "arbitrary" willing. Furthermore, being self-conscious and self-critical, it can decide what would be good and proper, and so is capable of selecting what is morally right. Even so, it is not fully free unless and until it can carry out its choice in actual practice.

Human beings are social animals. To be able to will anything at all they must at least be alive and they begin life as infants needing care and protection by their parents and, as they grow to adulthood, requiring nurture and education to acquaint them with the code of morals customary in the society to which they belong. It is in the family that these needs are provided. Indeed, as Hegel was acutely aware, morality itself is a social product, being the regulation of conduct essential to the elimination of conflict and the coordination of behavior among the members of a community. It follows that the conditions of carrying out in practice the free choices of individuals can be provided only by social institutions. They are thus the essential means to the realization of freedom, and the resulting order of society is what Hegel calls *Sittlichkeit* (a term difficult to translate – the nearest English equivalent is probably "customary morality"). This, he says, is the ethical substance, the unity of individuality and universality – the substance of freedom. Customary morality is the conduct (the modification of instinctive and impulsive behavior) that, in the course of nurture and education has become "second nature."

The institutions required by *Sittlichkeit* are first the family; then the forms of association involved in the supply of material needs: commerce and exchange, with all that their regulation and organization require (such as corporations, professional associations, craft guilds – and in our day labour unions – police and administration) – what Hegel calls Civil Society (*bürgerliche Gesellschaft*); finally the institutions of government: legislative, executive and judicial, the state proper, enacting and administering the laws that maintain order and regulate the relations between the various distinct functions within civil society and coordinate them with that of the family. The state is the unification and reconciliation of the family with civil society, as the objective realization of identity in difference. The whole body of these institutions is to be judged as to their functioning and appropriateness according to the efficiency with which they facilitate the carrying out in practice of free choices, which is impossible without them. Free action, however, is not completely genuine unless the members of these institutions accept and approve of their rules and interrelations, identifying themselves with them,[a] In the first place as defining and actualizing their personalities (e.g., as the head of a family, the member of a profession, an official of the administration, etc.), and in the second place especially, as so defined, with the nation as a whole. The aims and purposes of the individual are identified with those of the institutions of which he or she is a member, and neither can his or her free will be carried into practice nor can the aims of the institutions be realized except through the participation and cooperation of their members. In the institutions of *Sittlichkeit*, therefore, the particular

---

[a] This does not exclude the right to criticize the status quo, a right essential to "belonging" to an institution by its members, who are essentially self-reflective and self-critical.

and the universal unite – apart from the social order the free will of the individual is not realizable. *Sittlichkeit*, says Hegel, is freedom.

As final evidence of Hegel's devotion to individual freedom as realizable only in political order let me quote the decisive paragraph:

> The state is the actuality of concrete freedom. But concrete freedom consists in this, that personal individuality and its peculiar interests not only achieve their complete development and gain explicit recognition for their right (as they do in the sphere of the family and civil society) but, for one thing, they also pass over of their own accord into the interest of the universal, and, for another thing, they know and will the universal; they recognize it as their own substantive mind; they take it as their end and aim and are active in its pursuit. The result is that the universal does not prevail or achieve completion except along with particular interests and through the co-operation of particular knowing and willing; and individuals do not live for their own ends alone, but in the very act of willing these they will the universal in the light of the universal and their activity is consciously aimed at none but the universal end. The principle of modern states has prodigious strength and depth because it allows the principle of subjectivity to progress to its culmination in the extreme of self-subsistent personal particularity, and yet at the same time brings it back to the substantive unity and so maintains this unity in the principle of subjectivity itself.[a]

I think I have said enough to establish that Hegel conceived freedom positively, as the social milieu which enables people to carry out their reasonable intentions with the greatest of ease and the least obstruction.

---

[a]*Philosophie des Rechts*, 260 (Knox's translation). Hegel says that "the state is the actuality of the ethical Idea." (ibid. 257). For him, the Idea is the concrete universal in its final culmination - the identity of subjective and objective – the whole, which is the truth. So his reference to the universal here is to the state as a whole, including family, civil society and government, as they are unified and organized by the constitution; and his point is that in actualizing freedom in concrete objectivity it at the same time realizes the private interests of its citizens. Hegel insists on the interdependence of the universal and particular throughout the social order, emphasizing the dependence on the individual contribution of each and all its members for the success of the whole society in achieving its objectives (as, for instance, the supply of material needs depends on the efforts of individual entrepreneurs and craftsmen), which at the same time serves their own particular interests. The identity of private and public interest amounts to what Rousseau called the General Will - the will of the people to realize a common good, at once the aim of the citizen and of the state.

This is possible only with the cooperation and concerted activity of fellow citizens in rationally organized institutions, which together constitute a democratic state. His political philosophy, therefore, so far from legitimizing totalitarianism, is one of the most profound and convincing analyses of how democracy is actualized and what it should be.

Adam Smith, Utilitarianism, Hegel and Marx

In the mid-eighteenth century Rousseau and Hume were contemporaries; but Hume's declaration in his Treatise of Human Nature that "reason is and ought only to be the slave of the passions and can never pretend to any other office than to serve and obey them" had influence that extended far into the future. His friend, Adam Smith apparently took this assertion seriously, for in his initiatory work The Wealth of Nations he assumes that the predominating human motive is the urge to fulfill all natural desires, which will inevitably determine the outcome of economic production, supply and demand, which if left to themselves, without interference from politicians, will so regulate the economic process, through the checks and balances of operative forces and "the higgling of the market" as to produce a compromise of interests. "A hidden hand", he maintained, would so adjust these mutual interests that general satisfaction is achieved. This contention led to the advocacy of the political policy of laissez faire – that has persisted, at periodical intervals, to the present day – producing nowadays the most dire effects.

Hume's contention further influenced Bentham and the Utilitarians who followed him, so that they came to consider the predominant aim of all human action to be the pursuit of pleasure and the ultimate objective of social organization to be the achievement of the greatest pleasure of the greatest number. John Stuart Mill, writing on Liberty, maintained that the law should do no more than prevent the pursuit of pleasure by each individual from interfering with the free activity of seeking a similar end by others; and in general the combined effect of these tendencies was to encourage and require of governments, a *laissez faire* policy.

In economics this led to allowing producers free range to make as much money as possible and entrenched the over-riding profit motive among entrepreneurs, who did all they could to produce with as little as possible cost to themselves and to induce consumers to buy their stocks at the most attractive prices, seeking the profit indispensable to the survival of their business. Consumers, accordingly, at the same time were encouraged to seek to acquire possessions and goods to the full extent of their means (and beyond).

Following Locke's teaching, the belief prevailed that men were born free and had natural rights to liberty, life and the pursuit of happiness (as the preamble of the Constitution of the United States declared), and the American dream was engendered impelling everybody to seek to acquire all such amenities as were available.

The seeds were thus planted of a culture of consumerism in which shopping becomes a desirable pastime and acquisitiveness a common characteristic, while the entrepreneurs who produced goods and services, seek through advertising their wares, with the help of the most advanced psychological techniques, to persuade customers to buy, offering them discounts, free gifts, and apparent savings, which are for the most part deceptive, for no such offerings are made except with the aim of increasing profits. The disastrous effects of this culture have become evident in the present century, and will concern us in a later chapter.

Hegel had read the German translations of the works of Sir James Steuart and Adam Smith, and he was keenly aware of the problem presented by the development of industrialism and capitalism in the modern state consequent upon the division of labour. He was troubled by the fact, of which he became persuaded that the wealth of modern nations accrued only at the cost of the poverty of the working class. "Factories and manufacturers base their existence on the misery of a class", he writes; and again: "...condemns a multitude to a raw life and to dullness in labour and poverty, so that others can amass fortunes."[10] This arises because the division of labour necessary for the greater efficiency of modern manufacturing processes condemns the labourer to ever more dull, monotonous repetition for low wages. On the one hand, the accumulation of wealth is the natural method of the development of individuality among the members of Civil Society, and it has an inevitable tendency to increase without limitation. On the other hand, this occurs only at the expense of the impoverishment of the working class (Cf. *Realphilosophie* II, 231-2). To this problem Hegel could find no solution in terms of his own philosophical analysis of the modern state.

It is probable that passages like these in Hegel's writing influenced Karl Marx in his effort to resolve the problem of the exploitation of the working class by advocating Communism and the "dictatorship of the proletariat," preliminary to the eventual withering away of the state, when (in Engels' words) "government over persons is replaced by the administration of things and the direction of the processes of production."

There can be little doubt that Marx's primary motive was humanitarian. His aim was to emancipate the workers from exploitation by capitalist producers and the consequent misery of poverty. In practice, after the Russian revolution of 1917, this objective became distorted and the Soviet regime under Stalin was corrupted into a ruthless, barbarous and virtually imbecile tyranny, as is depicted in Aleksandr Solzhenitsyn's *Gulag Archipelago*.

After Stalin's death, this rabid tyranny was gradually ameliorated until Gorbachov introduced *glasnost* with the probable aim of establishing a more civilized form of socialism. That, if it was his intention, was prevented by the take-over by Boris Yeltsin and the total collapse of the Soviet system.

The outcome has been the expansion of globalized capitalism and the growth trans-national corporations with the consequent encouragement of unrestrained consumerism that, with the phenomenal expansion of the world population, threatens to exhaust the Earth's resources, while the vast emissions of greenhouse gases from industrial plants and the consumption of fossil fuels is causing rapidly advancing global warming with the threat of calamitous climate change.   Today   the prognostication of "the end of history" may well be credible, unless urgent steps are taken to counteract and remedy the deleterious processes that threaten contemporary civilization.

NOTES

[1] See p.13 above.

[2] T.H. Green, *Lectures on Political Obligation* (London, Longman, Green and Co.) 1924), p. 123f.

[3] Cf. Peter P. Nicholson, *The Political Philosophy of the British Idealists* (Cambridge, Cambridge University Press, 1990), Study VI, section 2, and B. Bosanquet, *The Philosophical Theory of the State* (London, Macmillan, 1899-1925).

[4] R.M. MacIver, *The Modern State* (London, Oxford University Press, 1926-1950), p. 200.

[5] A.D. Lindsay, *The Modern Democratic State* (Oxford, Oxford University Press,. 1943-1955), Ch. X.

[6] Cf. *The Philosophical Theory of the State*, Ch.VIII.

[7] Ernest Barker, *Reflections on Government* (Oxford, Oxford University Press, 1942), Pt. I, Ch.I, pp. 18-19.

[8] Ibid.

[9] Op cit., p.36.

[10] *Realphilosophie* II, 275 and 238, quoted by Schlomo Avneri in Hegel's *Theory of the Modern State* (Cambridge, Cambridge University Press, 1972), p. 96.

3. Democracy and Secularism

There is yet another feature of democracy that must be considered and discussed: one which at the present time is having significantly ominous effects and is, consequently, of special importance. It is the relation between religion and politics, the necessity that the latter remain strictly secular and that the former refrain from intrusion into affairs of state.

The specific concerns of religion are belief in God, obedience to divine commands, sin and repentance, divine forgiveness and love, and life after death. Of course different religions and denominations differ with respect to details, but anything other than the matters listed above are at best secondary for every religion. The concerns of politics, on the other hand, are restricted to the means and conditions of living on Earth and the regulation of human relationships relevant to them. Politicians (as such) cannot and ought not to try to concern themselves with anything else. They cannot in any way determine by law the religious beliefs (or lack of them) of their constituents, because people's religious beliefs are subjective and largely emotional; if they are to be sincere they cannot be enforced; and any attempt to enforce them can only result in unjustifiable, tyrannous persecution. Likewise, politics cannot be concerned with divine law, only with secular law as required by the state, nor can politics be in any way concerned with divine forgiveness, nor about an afterlife. Consequently, the affairs of state and its legislation must and can only legitimately be secular.

Furthermore, while religion is a matter of personal conviction, politics and secular law can take cognizance only of overt actions, irrespective of the beliefs that prompt them. Criminal law can appeal only to one motive, fear of punishment. Civil law is concerned only with recognized rights and claims based upon them. Neither can influence the motives of action or compel respect for moral obligation or devotion to moral ideals. Religion, on the other hand, imposes an absolute moral code, and different religions acknowledge different codes. For instance, Catholicism forbids all forms of artificial contraceptives and most emphatically abortion, whereas other religions may give priority to the safety of the pregnant woman and to the prevention of lethal diseases such as AIDS. For a secular government to attempt rigidly to enforce on everybody any rules of this kind would result only in unjustifiable persecution of those who seek to conform to other principles. The function of secular law in a democracy is not to enforce any absolute morality but to maintain and ensure justice among a diverse population.[a] Genuinely democratic government, therefore, must be secular and must maintain strict separation of politics from religious dogma.

Democracy, moreover, is in principle government representing all the people, who are distributed among many denominations, it cannot favour one in preference to others without abandoning religious toleration, for religious convictions are not simply personal opinions but are unconditional moral commitments, which the civil and criminal law cannot reach, and the fear of punishment for infringement cannot affect. If democracy is government by the people, it can only mean all the people; and, if the people include many religions and denominations, all are entitled on an equal footing to civil and political rights. To give preference to the practice of any particular cult at the expense of others would then be an injustice, so that in a genuine democracy strict secularism is the only permissible course. This does not mean that what some have called "orthodox secularism" and others (some Catholics) have identified as implicit atheism is what liberal democracy requires from its legislators

---

[a] Cf. Clifford Langley in *The Tablet*, 7 May, 2005: "This is becoming a familiar debate for Catholic electors and politicians to have, albeit somewhat awkwardly as the Church's official teaching has not yet reached a mature appraisal of what democracy demands. It often sounds as if it only respects the democratic process when it produces results it agrees with. But there is a more fundamental objection even than that to the claim that the civil and criminal law must invariably be moulded in accordance with the moral law (which we might call the absolutist position). It concerns enforceability, and the viability and integrity of the criminal justice system. The traditional priority of that system is not the imposing of a particular morality; it is about securing justice, with all that that implies."

and jurists. Any such imposition would be on a par with religious persecution. All that is required is that the effect of political action should never give undue advantage to any organized religious sect at the expense of others (or *vice versa*, put some sect or sects at a disadvantage in comparison with the rest).

The presupposition of the need for secularism in politics seems to be that religion is a matter of faith (belief without evidence), of conformity to the exhortations of selected persons (prophets) who have in the past recorded what they declared to be the Word of God. Obedience to or violation of these injunctions are rewarded or punished (as the case requires) by divine intervention. In politics, on the contrary, the legislator has no assured access to divine revelation nor is divine intervention at his disposal. All the legislator is called upon and is able to do is to pronounce rules that human reason dictates will facilitate the pursuits of everyday life and enforce them by practicable sanctions.

This contrast is liable to give rise to difficulties. Democratic politicians ought to respect the wishes of the majority both in the country and in the legislature, even if it favors measures which particular denominations may denounce. In consequence, legislators who happen to belong to a denomination that rejects a contemplated law will find themselves in a dilemma. In such cases questions will inevitably arise what the proper democratic attitude ought to be, what role the Churches should adopt in a democratic society, and how secularism can properly be maintained by the state concerned. This problem emerged in the history of the development of the democratic tradition in Europe, largely as a result of the Reformation and the wars of religion.

As has been noted, the historical development of democracy subsequent to the Ancient civilizations of Greece and Rome began in England as far back as *Magna Carta* and the first parliament set up by Simon de Montford. But more effectively it was established in consequence of the conflict between Charles I and his parliamentary opponents which led to the British Civil War, the confused events of that period and of the Commonwealth, and the eventual settlement of the Glorious Revolution of 1688. The Civil War was as much a war to achieve religious toleration as to establish the authority of Parliament and limit that of the King.

A struggle for political power between Church and State, however, dates back much further to the early Middle Ages, when Pope and Emperor vied for dominance each over the other. At that time the religion of Western Europe was Catholic and there were no other denominations. The distinction between the secular and the divine was drawn by the religious authority itself, and was recognized by both contestants, the rivalry being only for priority, which the Popes finally established for themselves. It was only after the Reformation and the wars of religion that ideas of the Rights of Man (Natural Rights) came to be widely advocated, in opposition to such doctrines as the Divine Right of Kings. The altercation was largely between the dictates of reason and the promptings of faith, despite the assurances given by religious thinkers like Thomas Aquinas that there was actually no conflict between them and that Natural Law was both rational and divine. The sixteenth century political philosophers, however, while they took over the doctrine of Natural Law, as we have noted, stressed its rational rather than its divine character.

The Reformation led to a proliferation of religious denominations: Lutheranism, Calvinism, Puritanism, Quakerism, Episcopalianism, as well as the longstanding organizations of Roman Catholicism and Eastern Orthodoxy. The protracted wars of religion, with their intolerances and massacres, culminating in the widespread devastation of the Thirty Years War, left Europe exhausted and its people longing for peace and tolerance. Spinoza pointed out that the attempt to enforce religious belief only converted otherwise law-abiding citizens into criminals. Genuine religious conviction is not affected by penalties imposed by political authorities, which at most can only impinge upon overt actions seeming to indicate religious belief (at times misleadingly, as when, for example, a refusal to eat shell-fish, prompted perhaps by nothing other than distaste, is taken, as it was by the Inquisition in the sixteenth century, to signify Jewish adherence to Mosaic dietary law).

Religious persecution that had so long been wounding and destroying the lives of private persons, and in England had been the cause of sedition and mayhem throughout the reigns of the Tudor Queens, Mary and Elizabeth I, had led to the Popish plot to blow up the King in Parliament in 1605 with the capture and condemnation of Guy Fawkes. Peace-loving citizens as well as governments became wearied with the effects of religious persecution, but it was not until after the Enlightenment and (in Britain) Catholic Emancipation, that freedom of conscience gradually came to be regarded as a necessary principle of democratic government. It seemed logical, therefore, to draw a strict division between religion and politics, to regard civil administration as essentially secular and to exclude from it any appeal to religious dogma.

On the Continent of Europe it was the French Revolution and Napoleon's conquests that spread the idea and the philosophical tradition of popular government more generally. And the philosophical argument had been as much inspired by the Ancient traditions and by Humanism as by religious disputes. Accordingly, the European continental idea of democracy was considerably infused with the notions of the Enlightenment and tended to be anti-clerical and secular.

During much the same period under the influence of the Enlightenment and the professed ideals of the French Revolution, at least initially, all religions were regarded as free and equal; Napoleon in effect secularized France giving full citizenship to Jews and producing a view of religion as a private affair outside the province of politics. His conquests spread the practice, and henceforth at least in the western countries of Europe secularism was tacitly admitted, even in traditionally Catholic countries, like Spain and Italy. Shortly before this, Moses Mendelsohn in Germany had advocated the separation of religious from civic activity and had begun a movement in that country tending in the same direction, which eventually led to Reform Judaism, the effect of which was the recognition of Jews as citizens on an equal basis with the members of other faiths and – in Britain, the Netherlands and elsewhere – their admission on an equal footing to governmental office. In some other countries it took longer to establish complete freedom of religious belief, and anti-semitism remained a savage and bitter ingredient in some eastern European regimes, coming to an execrable climax in the Nazi holocaust.

Although the original motivation of the Pilgrim Fathers was escape from religious persecution, secularism in political administration was explicitly accepted by the founders of the United States. Thomas Jefferson disestablished the Episcopal Church in Virginia in 1786, declaring that coercion in matters of religion was "sinful and tyrannical" and other states followed suit. The First Amendment of the Constitution forbids the making of laws establishing religion or prohibiting its free exercise, thus legally separating the state from religion, making religious belief a private affair to be left to the conscience of the believer, and Article VI, 3, abolished religious tests for office in the federal government. It was clear to the founders of the new federation that it could only rely on the loyalty of its members as long as it refrained from giving precedence to any one denomination.

In neither of the English speaking nations, however, has secularism been observed with absolute strictness. In Great Britain the Church of

England is the established Church with the monarch as its titular head and its senior bishops sitting in the House of Lords, where they will continue to sit as members of the second legislative chamber until Parliament reforms its structure and method of election or appointment. In America nobody objects to the frequent announcement and publicization of the national slogans, "In God we trust" and "One Nation under God." Nevertheless, (at least until recently) the accepted view of political action as such has been that it is secular and unaffected by religious dogma.

Among the Islamic nations tradition had always given prominence to religious requirements and secularism was not a notable feature until Napoleon's invasion of Egypt in 1798. He brought with him scientists and scholars from the west who introduced modern ideas foreign to the Middle East, which henceforth proved attractive. He also declared publicly that he had not come to destroy the Islamic faith, in effect, introducing the notion, of secularization. The idea caught on; Islamic notables visited western capitals, especially Paris, and studied western military and natural sciences, returning with an urge to modernize Islamic regimes. Muhammad Ali, the first Pasha of Egypt, revolutionized and transformed the economic structure of the country from agrarianism in the direction of industrialism, developing the cotton industry, extending irrigation and advancing agricultural production. He adopted French methods of military training for the Egyptian army and separated his own dictatorial administration from the influence of the Islamic jurists imposing a secularism that was not traditional but was alien and unfamiliar. These measures were foreign to and incompatible with the customs of the people and tore the social structure of the country to pieces, so that while they secularized the administration they provoked a reaction among the people and the clergy that later had significant and drastic effects of which we shall take note in Chapter V.

At the same time, the Ottoman Empire, which, in its hey-day had extended from southern Spain to the borders of Afghanistan, at the beginning of the nineteenth century, was in decline, and several of its leading personalities sought to modernize it and to adopt western ideas and methods. Some of them were sent to western Europe as ambassadors and diplomats and avidly absorbed the culture of the west, becoming convinced that the Ottoman Empire could only survive in the modern world if it were centralized, if it modernized its army, and treated all faiths alike within its dominions; in short, unless its administration became secular. These efforts, however, resulted rather in subordinating regimes to the growing powers of Western Europe than intrinsically transforming Islamic traditions (although Islam had been more tolerant of other religions in the Middle Ages than had Christianity). The nineteenth century changes were imitative rather than indigenous and their eventual effect was to subject Middle Eastern countries (Egypt and Persia in particular) to western powers, so that, especially after the cutting of the Suez Canal, they became more or less colonized by Britain and France. In Persia (the present-day Iran) Russian influence, along with British, was strong, both before and after the Communist revolution. The consequences were mixed: in part tending towards secularization, and in part provoking resentment and hostility.

After the defeat of the Ottoman Empire by the western powers in the First World War, Kemal Ataturk set up a national Turkish state, establishing it on a secular model and ruthlessly excluding all influence from the Islamic religious orders. He did so at an atrocious cost of ethnic cleansing, massacring Armenian and other non-Turkish sections of the population to eliminate foreign (and incidentally Christian) elements. This drastic secularization of a Muslim nation was at one and the same time attractive to other Middle Eastern dictators and a glaring example to the rest of the Muslim world of the danger to religion of modernization and national secularism.

In Egypt, during the earlier decades of the twentieth century, the British introduced some institutions of democratic government, but they were largely cosmetic, although there were influential Egyptians who favored the secular type of political order and thought that the western model could be combined with an Islamic base, modified appropriately, to bring it up to date. Others believed that Islam could be modernized without adopting western institutions and could be established on the foundation of Shariah law. Yet others, however, were firmly opposed altogether to secularization.

Similar moves were made in Iran to introduce a representative parliamentary constitution and convert the Shah into a constitutional monarch. But the interference of the Russians and the British, who were interested in Iranian oil production, weakened and to a great extent nullified these developments. When the Shah was eventually expelled by the Islamic revolution, the country was ruled by a divided authority, in part secular, but in part by a more powerful and effective religious dictatorship of the Ayatollas.

Meanwhile, among Jewish communities, Zionism was organizing and agitating for a Jewish homeland, which the British, who held the mandate over Palestine after the Great War, promised in the Balfour Declaration. Zionism was essentially secular, many of its supporters being Marxists and agnostics who were anti-religious. Reformed Judaism, on the other hand, was secularist in a different sense, preferring in the main to continue as a tolerated denomination in democratic states such as America, France, and Britain, and in general holding aloof from Zionism, although not openly opposed to it. There was, however, also a strong body of orthodox Jewry who rejected Zionism altogether on the religious ground that the Old Testament prophets had foretold that not until the Messiah had come would he lead the Israelites back to the Promised Land. The chief Zionist argument for an Israeli state, however, was as a haven from the murderous persecution that Jews had suffered throughout the entire period of the Diaspora, especially in eastern Europe and Russia; and the Nazi holocaust strengthened this argument so obviously that after the state of Israel had been established, and millions of Jews had immigrated into it, the Orthodox element, while not abandoning their opposition to secularism, found themselves involved in the politics of the new state, giving them unintended influence which could support their religious convictions, but which has had significant, and unsalutary international consequences.

Thus, historically, while in the west the principles requiring secularism in politics have gradually come to be recognized and have come to be seen as appropriate to genuinely democratic government, further east such secularism as has been adopted has largely been imposed from without, is generally peripheral, and has had shallow roots.

Western democracies have realized that if religious doctrines were allowed to prevail in legislation the enacted laws would inevitably provoke conscientious objection among those whose religion was at variance with the doctrines concerned, so that either the law would have to make provision for exemptions from its application, or freedom of conscience would be infringed and those who disobeyed the law on conscientious grounds would be victimized. In the first case the law would be strictly unenforceable and in the second it would be unjust; so it would be bad law. The intrinsic idea of democracy, the sovereignty of the popular will, is freedom, the most essential element of which is freedom of conscience. It follows that, if religious dogma encroaches upon political decision, the very essence of democracy is in jeopardy. The appropriate democratic course should be for the opinion of the majority of elected representatives to prevail, and for those who object to it to campaign peacefully aiming to change popular opinion sufficiently to bring the majority into agreement with their point of view.

To the philosophers of the 19th and 20th Centuries, who thought of democracy only in the context of separate Western countries, this issue did not seem to make so urgent a demand; but it tends to loom larger today because, as is to be explained presently, the establishment of secularism itself excites a reaction among the religious devout, giving rise to all kinds of fundamentalism, the political affects of which high-light more emphatically the question (to be raised in the following chapters) how far the democratic tradition, as hitherto conceived, is currently true of present practice or can be made so more universally.

Nevertheless, the early twentieth century thinkers clearly recognized the necessary limitation of civil government to concern with overt behavior. Barker had demonstrated that rational discussion at the diverse levels of political and legal activity was the essence of democratic practice, the participants in which are assumed to respect the opposing opinions and to be open to conviction by cogent argument. Religious belief is not so easily influenced, if at all, by philosophical persuasion. T.H. Green and Bosanquet had argued that the resulting modification of political policies by public criticism, if not entirely identical with the real general will of the community, would at least approximate to it; and that it would, in consequence, converge with the dictates of the conscience of the individual citizen. But if the individual's conscience is directed by his or her religious belief, how does this doctrine conform to the principle of political secularism, which, as presented above, should be a necessary feature of all political activity, especially of genuine democracy? If secular policies run counter to religious pronouncements, how is freedom of conscience to be preserved and subjection to some form of authoritarianism to be avoided, either religious on the one hand, or political on the other? Might secular discussion so neutralize religious differences that compromise can be reached with which all religious consciences can be reconciled? Or if, as is normally the case, religious requirements may not be over-ruled by any utilitarian consideration, how is the secular law to be framed so that it can be obeyed without violating the religious beliefs of some or all of its subjects?

It would seem that the only solution to this problem is for people to agree that secular policies enacted by democratic governments should be decided by majority vote, and that laws should be so framed that, while they permitted practices favored by the majority (say, contraception or abortion), they did not impose them on others who disapproved for religious or other conscientious reasons. Such laws would be permissive rather than prohibitive, yet a rule of this kind should not exclude the possibility of prohibiting practices, whether required by religious custom or not, which are deemed to be unjust, generally harmful, or unnecessarily cruel (for instance, thugism, the method of slaughtering animals required by the dietary laws of some religions, the prohibition of the use of condoms to prevent the spread of HIV infection, or the unfair favoring of persons of a particular denomination in official actions involving conflicts of interests). The question of strict political secularism is thus complicated and shot through with difficulties, and the maintenance of freedom of conscience presents problems that cannot easily or straightforwardly be solved.

Suggestions such as we have made above, moreover, do not immediately solve the problem of democratizing existing regimes that subordinate the secular power to religious authority (as in Iran), or that retain all political power in the hands of religious officials, Ayatollas, et al. And if the majority of the population of such a state approves of its religious authoritarianism, the question will arise whether "democratization" of whatever kind is really appropriate.

We have persisted, however, in the assumption that democracy is the ultimately desirable form of government and that those regimes that are not now democratic should, by whatever means possible, be developed towards democracy; so that even if this objective has not as yet been attained it should remain the final aim of political evolution. Whether or not its achievement would signal the end of history need not concern us, rather than whether democracy or some other governmental arrangement is the best for all mankind. What the alternatives might be is far from obvious. Dictatorships of all kinds (even if allegedly benevolent) seem altogether unacceptable, if only because they obstruct the beneficial development of personal character that proceeds from the exercise of free choice. They also leave the decision exclusively to the dictator (if benevolent) as to what ultimately consists in the common good, a decision that is never infallible, and which can only be reached legitimately by genuine discussion and criticism of diverse individual opinions. Clearly, what is desirable is that the necessary forms of human intercourse indispensable to organized social conduct, without which "the bare needs of life" cannot be obtained nor "the good life" assured, should be regulated in a manner that is just and equitable to all concerned. And this has been the goal to which all social reformers and all political philosophers have always sought to advance; the minimal conditions of which are, surely, the rule of law, equality of persons before the law, equality of opportunity, freedom of speech and of legitimate association and above all of conscience. To these matters we shall return at a later stage.

It is not easily discernible how these aims can be achieved while observing the rule that the political authority and political procedures should be strictly secular in character, ensuring at the same time, freedom of religion and freedom of conscience; nor how a dominant religious sect can be prevented from unduly influencing the government of a country in which that sect can assemble a majority of voters. Northern Ireland is a case in point, where for the most part religious denomination has determined political allegiance, the majority of nationalists who demand a united Ireland being Catholic and those favoring union with Great Britain being Protestant. Attempts to persuade these parties to submit to democratic procedures rather than to resort to para-militarism and violence for decades have failed, with exceedingly detrimental effects on the welfare of the population, as well as serious obstacles to the establishment of democratic government. In Israel the problem has become even more intractable and will receive our attention at a later stage.

In recent decades western democratic countries have admitted immigrants, either as asylum seekers from regimes that violate human rights or as economic migrants seeking more favourable living conditions, who adhere to different and non-Christian faiths. Problems have arisen of maintaining secularism and at the same time preserving religious freedom when the religious practices of these faiths conflict with secular requirements. Such problems are proving increasingly difficult to circumvent, and as yet no clear solution seems to be in sight.

The examples we have adduced may be instructive, but they do not assist much in determining principle. We are still faced with the problem, whether, or how, to maintain secularism in the affairs of the state, while ensuring the liberties which genuine democracy professes to secure. As will appear later, the unprecedented spread and activities of fundamentalists in all three of the major Abrahamic religions has intensified the problem and made it more acute than ever before; but this is a subject large enough to provide material for more than one book and its discussion in this essay may best be consigned to a separate chapter.

Failure to resolve this problem will affect the question whether the traditional vision of democracy is viable at the present time. We seek to decide to what extent contemporary practice conforms to principle as traditionally conceived, and clearly secularism is an important element implicit in the traditional ideal; yet it is not apparent how this particular element can be made compatible, under the conditions prevailing in the twenty-first century, with the multi-racial and multi-denominational populations that are developing in several western democracies, in many cases as a result of religious intolerance in other countries elsewhere. Nor is it easily apparent how the invasion of secular politics by contemporary varieties of religious fundamentalism can be checked or prevented.

4. Democracy and Fundamentalism

A t the beginning of the twenty-first century a new and sinister development has arisen, quite unexpected and unforeseen in the earlier half of the twentieth century a growing insinuation of religious extremisms into the process of government. Nowadays the principle of political secularism is becoming compromised, especially in America, by the rise of Christian fundamentalism and Evangelism, which are exerting an undue influence on political activity (the First Amendment to the American Constitution notwithstanding), causing tensions and dilemmas for politicians both there and elsewhere in connection with such issues as the legalization of abortion and euthanasia, which conflict with the doctrine of the Catholic Church, as well as affecting other policies in undesirable and dangerous ways. Candidates who stand for political election find themselves in a quandary if the Church to which they belong seeks to exclude those who concur with legislation condemned by its dogma while the political party for which the candidate is standing supports the measures obnoxious to their Church (as, for instance, has occurred in the United States where some Catholic bishops have refused communion to those who vote for the legalization of abortion).

The very growth of modern democracy and its involvement of secularism has itself generated in all three of the major Abrahamic religions (Judaism, Christianity, and Islam) a reaction – a virtual backlash – which has developed into fundamentalisms of extreme and irrational forms which, in various ways, impinge deleteriously upon democracy over much of the world. Modern democracy, as we noted in earlier chapters, has largely been developed from the doctrines of Natural Law and natural rights as well as the rationalism that characterized the Age of

Enlightenment. This again was closely connected with the Copernican revolution in science and the consequent contrast between faith and reason high-lighted by the dispute between Galileo and the Inquisition. Natural Law had earlier been regarded as at once the Law of God and the law of reason; but henceforth the two seemed to be at loggerheads – a conflict further exacerbated two centuries later by Darwin's theory of the origin of species, which cast doubt upon the Biblical description of God's creation of heaven and earth and their inhabitants. Laws of nature henceforth took on a new meaning: they were scientific generalizations supported by experiment and observation, and although many scientists and other thinkers might still view them as divine ordinances, this assumption (as Laplace's famous answer to Napoleon's question expressed) was no longer necessary. The rational approach of science came generally to be regarded as Modernism, of which secularism was a characteristic feature and which had, among other things, stimulated the Higher Criticism of the Bible by theologians themselves. This gave rise to what is known as Modernist Christianity, assuming a liberal attitude to biblical interpretation, which views the sacred writings as historical documents to be judged in the light of the common beliefs of the peoples at the time when they were written, and accepts large parts of them as metaphorical and symbolic and only to a limited extent literal versions of the truth. Modern democracy is a typical product of the same rationalist spirit as this liberal modernism and the requirement of secularism in politics is a natural outcome.

To a great number of religious devotees such Modernism and the pervasive secularism accompanying it is anathema, and by some of them it is regarded as nothing less than the work of the Devil, threatening the very existence of religious faith. Reason itself, to such people and the sects that they make up, has become a sacrilege and is regarded as demonic. They see it as the way in which Satan corrupts humanity and as the form of satanic temptation that begets the modernism which alienates people from the divine command and the worship of the true God. In its stead they revere the statement in the Bible of what they regard as God's will for humanity and His divine law. The Bible is understood literally by such believers and its prophesies are not interpreted as symbolic or metaphorical. The historical chronicles and miraculous events it records are accepted without criticism, regardless of inconsistencies and apparent contradictions, no further corroborative evidence being called for. The higher criticism, which the rational approach of the Enlightenment had encouraged, is seen as heretical and mere blasphemy.

As we have already observed, Zionism among the Jews is primarily secular and practical, seeking to establish a haven and protection from the atrocious persecution to which Jews in the Diaspora have suffered for centuries. But a number of the orthodox oppose it on fundamentalist grounds, based on the prophesies of Old Testament writers which foretold that only after the Messiah had come would the Hebrew tribes be restored to the Promised Land. These ultra-orthodox Jews condemned Zionism as apostasy, even accusing the Zionists of so deeply offending God that He had brought the holocaust upon them as a punishment. Some of them even went so far as to identify the Zionists with the Nazis comparing them to Hitler. The cultivation of the Holy Land by the people in the kibbutzim was to these extremists an outrage and a defilement, the evil work of those who had rejected religion.

Others, however, also orthodox, believed that only in Eretz Yisroel could Judaism be practiced as it properly should be, whereas in exile it could only, as it were, be imitated. They immigrated into Israel to fulfill this aspiration, but at first held themselves aloof from the secular Zionists and took no part in state politics. At the same time some of the secular Zionists regarded settlement in Israel as itself having quasi-religious significance, believing that no more was needed to restore spirituality to Jewish life than simple presence in the Promised Land by its mere environmental influence.

Some of the less extreme orthodox Jews, while they considered the state alien to religious practice, had opposed Zionism and had condemned the Balfour Declaration; but after the horrors of the Nazi holocaust during World War II were prepared to go along with the Zionist movement so far as it provided a refuge for Jews fleeing from persecution; and they were willing to bargain with the government of Israel once the state had been established, to safeguard religious interests. Yet others would have nothing to do with politics, refusing to vote in elections or to visit government offices or to accept government money and assistance.

The ultra-orthodox group regarded the state of Israel and its secular politics as an abomination, but although they were by no means a negligible factor in the community, they were a minority, and many of the less orthodox simply held that political activity had no religious significance. They were prepared to take part in the political process so far as it helped to serve religious ends, at the same time viewing politics as a pollution from which they needed to purify themselves. When the Likud Party defeated the Labour Party in the 1977 election, having been at odds with it over its willingness to respect the United Nations ruling which forbad Jewish settlements on the West Bank, these orthodox Jews joined with Likud to form part of a coalition government

A body of extreme fundamentalist Israelis, in defiance of their own government as well as the United Nations, had launched a campaign to create settlements beyond the internationally recognized boundaries of Israel. At first this caused minor physical clashes between them and their own Israeli authorities. But the resistance of the latter was never very determined and the settlements were set up and multiplied in number. During the 1970s a diverse group, partly of orthodox rabbis, partly of secular Israelis planned to settle the whole of the West Bank. One of the rabbis declared that there could be no peace in the Middle East until the entire Eretz Yisroel had been settled by Israelis; and after it had come to power the Likud government pursued a deliberate policy of encouraging settlements in the Palestinian areas, creating well over a hundred.

The effect on Israeli relations with the Palestinians was foreseeably profound, as the Orthodox Jewish groups believed that any attempt at reconciliation was strictly forbidden by divine instruction (compare Samuel's admonishment to Saul to annihilate the Amalekites presenting it as God's command). Orthodox Jews were also associated with, and supported by, Jews in America, both those who were themselves orthodox and others who were reformed. This augmented the already strong Jewish lobby in the United States and more or less ensured continued support of the US administration for the state of Israel in its conflict with the Palestinians.

A considerable body of Jewish opinion basing itself on Biblical authority considers that God's promise to them of the Land of Israel gives them the legal right to occupy the whole of the territory of the ancient Israelite kingdoms, and that would involve a complete expulsion of the Palestinians. They claimed the right to settlement on the West Bank even when it was still part of the Kingdom of Jordan. Some of the fundamentalists who hold this position found allies among the more secularly inclined Zionists and formed a pressure group to prevent the Israeli government from conforming to the decisions of the United Nations which had declared such settlements illegal. The fundamentalists maintained that they were not subject to any law other than the Torah and that by settling in land now occupied by Palestinians they were setting the messianic redemption in progress. Their more secular allies understood the notion of redemption in a more political sense and sought to regard their aggressive policy as rooting Zionism more securely in Judaism. This group therefore constitutes a virtually insurmountable obstacle to any acceptable agreement between the warring parties, with the effect of stimulating more intractable hostility among the Palestinians and their Islamic supporters in other countries and promoting violence and terrorist action from people who have no other way of resisting encroachment on what they claim as their rightful possession.

Such Jewish fundamentalism blocks all progress towards peace in the Middle East (the Arab-Israeli conflict extends far beyond the borders of Israel), for the opposition of the extremists is not only to the Palestinians and to international efforts to bring about agreement, but just as much to their own secular government if it makes any moves towards reconciliation with the Palestinians. It is small wonder that among the Arab and other Muslim nations there is a considerable body of similar intransigence among those who vow to wipe Israel off the map and declare holy war against her and her allies.

The extremism and resistance to all rational negotiation by such fundamentalist groups makes them effectively unapproachable. Their conviction that they are subject to no law except the Torah deprives of meaning any appeal to International Law. There seems to be no way in which their intransigence can be overcome, and so far as such fundamentalists participate in politics, one is faced with a situation in which the problem of excluding religious dogma from influencing political procedures and action seems altogether insoluble. Their influence obstructs any moves towards religious toleration of other faiths, and with such stubborn convictions the democratic process of discussion becomes impossible.

Among Muslims fundamentalism has been intensified by the general reaction against modernism as well as by other more particular causes. Kemal Ataturk's ruthless secularization of Turkey, whose people he had molded into a new nation after the fall of the Ottoman Empire, was seen by many Muslims as a threat to their religion, although Turkey remains a Muslim nation to this day. The reforms of Muhammad Ali had pauperized the Egyptian fellahin and put strains on the social life and traditions of Egypt that evoked a hostile opposition, and the continued modernizing process advocated by some of their more westernized politicians, and pressures on the country exerted by British and French domination, strengthened that hostility further.

At first the modernization movement seemed to be succeeding. Many prominent Egyptians thought that nationalization was the secret of success in the west and sought to secularize their own government entirely, but their attempts at establishing a constitutional monarchy were limited by the dominance and oversight of the British, which, especially during the First World War, was much enhanced. The process continued and was salutary to the extent that in the Second World War it saved Egypt (and all Asia Minor) from invasion by and subjection to the ruthless racist dictatorship of Mussolini and Hitler. But after the war, resistance to British colonialism and French commercial interests increased and came to a head during the Suez Canal crisis. Muslim fundamentalist societies were formed and some of them have, more recently, resorted to terrorist tactics against European tourists. The Egyptian government tries to suppress these activities (if only because the Egyptian economy is largely dependent on tourism), but they continue underground and fundamentalism thrives in those religious circles which normally shun politics.

While in the early years of the twentieth century some Muslims favored secularism and strove to free their polity completely from religion, others felt strongly that western modernization would destroy their faith, as they believed it would do in Turkey. Some thought a modern state could be built on a Muslim foundation, going back, as they held, to basics; others rejected modernism in all its forms and wished to return to the Shariah.

In Persia (now Iran) the main Muslim sect is Shiite, whose doctrines have some affinity to those of Christianity. The Shiites believe that Muhammad's successor was illegitimate and that, had Muhammad, before his death, indicated who should take his place, it would have been his nearest male relative, Ali ibn Ali Talib, who eventually became the fourth Calif. The Shiites call him the First Imam, discounting the first three Caliphs as impostors. Ali was, however, assassinated in 661. His son Hasan is called the Second Imam, but he took no part in politics and died in Medina in 669. Ali's second son, Husain, was then acclaimed the Third Imam. He retired to Mecca where he sought sanctuary from the new Umayyad Caliph, who sent troops against him, annihilating him and a small band of followers, a tragedy that is annually remembered by the Shiites in a religious day of mourning. Husain's son Ali escaped the massacre and became the Fourth Imam, and his grandson, Muhammad, the Fifth. The line continued to the Eleventh Imam, who died in 874 in mysterious circumstances. It was not clear whether he had any descendants, but many believed that he had a son, who had gone into hiding to escape from the opposition of the Abbasid Caliph, and who was the Twelfth Imam. As time passed without any direct communication with the Twelfth Imam the belief grew that he did not (and would not) die. He became known as the Hidden Imam miraculously concealed by Allah. This so-called Occultation, it was believed, would end when the Hidden Imam eventually returned, before the Last Judgment, to inaugurate a reign of peace and justice (much as Christians believe in the resurrection and second coming of Jesus).

The hostility between the Caliphs and the Shiite religious leaders led the latter and their followers to abjure politics, so that traditionally the political authorities in Shiite regions are secular – a fact that later has had significant consequences. In the first half of the nineteenth century, Britain and Russia had gained special privileges in Persia for their merchants, exempting them from local law and tariffs, concessions that were detrimental to local industries. In the latter half of the century, Britain, seeking to improve communication with her empire in India, obtained the right to monopolize construction of telegraph lines and railways despite strong protestations from Muslim parties surrounding the Shah's court. These incursions by westerners aroused opposition from merchants and devout Shiites, who were supported by the legal scholars (the *ulema*). Many feared the western encroachment as a threat both to the regime and to the religion of the country. This discontent grew into an actual revolt, but the government suppressed it with considerable violence and forced many of the religious leaders into exile in the holy city of Najaf in Iraq.

In the early years of the twentieth century, a strong movement occurred in Iran to westernize the regime. Protestations from merchants against the disadvantages they experienced from high tariffs led to discontent and with the support of the *ulema* a demand was voiced for constitutional government. The Shah was persuaded to agree and a Majlis (parliament) was established under a constitution that required the Shah to seek its approval of all important decisions. Westernization of the regime continued, the Majlis proceeded to limit the powers of the clergy and secularization was advanced, in part by direct government action, and in part by the withdrawal from politics of those Shiites who saw the new developments as a threat to their religion, believing that such reforms could not be correctly accomplished in the absence of the Hidden Imam.

These constitutional changes in Iran were, however, hampered by interference from the western powers. Russia and Britain became alarmed when the Majlis appealed to the Americans for assistance. The Russians invaded the country in 1911 and closed down the Majlis for the next three years, so that many became disillusioned with the reform process, feeling that their attempt to modernize had been unrewarding.

During the First World War Russian and British troops occupied Iran, until, after the Communist revolution in 1917, the Russians withdrew and the British took their place. Russian interest in the country was, however, renewed not much later. Britain proceeded more or less to colonize Iran, British oil companies having gained concessions when oil had been discovered before the war. Discontent grew and anti-British feeling was rife. Reza Khan, an army commander, overthrew the government and appealed for help to the Russians and the Americans to displace the British. Reza and some of the more secular-minded Iranians, feeling that they had become too dependent upon foreign influences, wished to set up a republic, but the religious faction objected, contending that that would be contrary to Islamic law; so Reza promised to govern in conformity with the Shariah if he became Shah. The Majlis gave in and he became the founder of the Pahlavi dynasty. Soon he managed to concentrate all power in his own hands and proceeded to modernize the country even more ruthlessly than Ataturk had done in Turkey. During the Second World War, however, the British considered Reza to be pro-German (indeed, some of his methods of government resembled those of Hitler and Stalin) and they forced him to abdicate. His son Muhammad who succeeded him ruled at first somewhat more moderately, but still made use of his father's secret police and was uncompromising and frequently as violent in suppressing any form of opposition.

The modernization conducted by the Pahlavi dynasty benefited only the wealthy, altogether neglecting the needs of the poorer agrarian mass of the population, who became increasingly aggrieved. There was widespread resentment against the prevalent foreign domination and the Tudeh party, led by Muhammad Mosaddeq, which emerged at this time, was socialistic and favored the Soviets, alarming the Americans who, in collusion with the British, plotted to get rid of Mosaddeq but failed. Nevertheless, the increasing discontent of the people and their resentment at foreign interference eventually led to an Islamic revolution that forced the Shah, despite American support, into exile, and brought the Grand Ayatollah Khomeini, whom the populace virtually idolized, into a dominant position in the country. President Carter's support of the Shah led to the identification of him and Americans in general as the Great Satan, by fundamentalist Muslims in Iran (and elsewhere), setting afoot an anti-western hatred among many Muslims that eventually spawned Al

Qaeda under the leadership of Osama bin Laden and resulted in the terrorist atrocity in the United States of September 11, 2001.

The religious beliefs that supported these developments were greatly influenced by the publications of two distinguished fundamentalist thinkers, Abdul Ala Mawdudi (a Pakistani who published his work in Egypt and the Egyptian Sayyid Qutb whom Mawdudi's writings had deeply impressed. Mawdudi feared that the overweening power of the western nations would destroy Islam. He believed that the absolute power of God should be accepted as the sole ruler and that only God's law was sovereign. Every state should be a theocracy in which God alone should make the laws and not men. God's law was revealed in the Koran from which no departure or to which no addition could rightfully be made. Neither the Caliph nor the people could be the actual rulers; all they could legitimately do was to administer the Shariah. In short, a truly Islamic state would be totalitarian. Democracy was a western invention not to be imitated or tolerated. The colonizing western nations were regarded as the powers of evil, appropriating to themselves what was God's authority. Mawdudi exhorted all Muslims to wage *Jihad* to secure the power to impose God's law on the whole world for the benefit of all humanity. This belief in the redeeming effect of Muslim victory over the infidels echoes the similar belief of orthodox Jews that the redemption of the entire world would be achieved with the complete settlement of the Holy Land by Israel as the prelude to the Messianic process.

Sayyid Qutb taught a similar doctrine. The colonization by the western powers in Egypt and the Middle East, and especially their support for Israel, seemed to him utterly evil. The pragmatic utilitarianism of the west appeared merely perverse. Secularism and all its works were to him utterly barbaric, a menace to religion and piety, which Muslims were morally obliged to combat at all costs. From the time of the Crusades to the present, Qutb saw a series of enemies bent on the destruction of the Muslim faith culminating today in the Western capitalist nations and their support for Zionism. This paranoia concerning Western secularism as a mortal danger to their religion and an international conspiracy to destroy it is common among fundamentalists, whether they be Muslim, Jewish, or Christian. Ayatollah Khomeini in Iran, much influenced by the writings of Mawdudi and Qutb, in many of his sermons and speeches spoke of a conspiracy of western imperialism of Marxists, Jews, and Christians to overwhelm Islam, a belief encouraged by the support given to the Pahlavi dictatorship by the Americans.

As with the Israeli insistence that the only valid law is the Torah, so the Islamic belief that, with the Shariah, the Koran alone should be obeyed, militates against the western idea of democracy and the Rule of Law among civilized nations. It elevates dictatorship and totalitarianism as the sole legitimate form of government and is a menace to the democratic ideal, whether as set out by the philosophers or as conceived by contemporary Americans as the universally desirable type of polity.

In the United States, in the early eighteenth century, the first Great Awakening led by the theologian and philosopher Jonathan Edwards[a] and the English Methodist minister George Whitefield was the first of a series of revivalist movements that have occurred periodically in that country; but not until recently have they impinged upon politics. The Awakening was a wave of religious emotionalism that swept through New England, with preachers, both old and new, tending to think of current events in eschatological terms as described in the Book of Revelation. This has been a characteristic of many subsequent revivalist movements which today threatens to have ominous consequences. The Great Awakening induced many to think of America as the Promised Land ("God's own country") and its inhabitants as a chosen people. The preacher Ebenezer Baldwin declared that the war of independence would inaugurate God's plan for His Kingdom which Christ would establish in America on His second coming. As the settlers of the east pushed westward beyond the Allegheny Mountains at the beginning of the nineteenth century a Second Great Awakening, led by preachers who gave expression to the frontiersmens' grievances against the governments in the east, was more political. The preachers spoke in a language that ordinary men could understand, appealing to the Bible as it was written, without learned commentary, and urging their parishioners to think for themselves. They stressed the egalitarian teaching of the New Testament by which the settlers' demands seemed justified, making little or no distinction between religion and politics.

Before the American Civil War, slavery generated among the Africans whom the slave trade had introduced an other-worldliness that expressed itself in spiritual hymns, which had no political significance at the time, but still inspire many southern Baptists, who, in the 1960s headed a significant political agitation led by Martin Luther King demanding civil rights for blacks. The Northerners had, in the Civil War, thought of themselves as cleansing the nation from its sinfulness and

---

[a] Not to be confused with the British Olympic record holder of the triple-jump.

sang of "the coming of the glory of the Lord", but the disappointment at the war's end, with the devastation it had caused and the problems of reconciliation with the southern states as well as those of subsequent growth and development in the north, produced disillusionment. A gloomy view of human nature produced a new form of fundamentalism called "premillennialism" based on the prophesies of the Book of Revelation, to the effect that a period of strife and warfare against the Anti-Christ would precede the Second Coming, when Jesus would institute a thousand years of peace and establish God's Kingdom. A more optimistic version, "postmillennialism", was the belief that matters would improve and that men would establish the peaceful and virtuous millennium before the Second Coming. Emphatic assertions of the literal truth of the Bible were associated with both these movements and gained widespread acceptance.

Twentieth century revivalist movements, of which there have been many and diverse, have mostly concentrated on converting people to greater piety and belief in the Gospel, they were characteristically conversionist. The converts claimed to be and boasted of being "born again" Christians. Billy Graham, an itinerant preacher, was one of the most successful, drawing huge crowds to his meetings, which ended with emotional scenes of numbers of his hearers confessing their conversion and change of life. In 1979 Jerry Falwell formed a movement that he called the Moral Majority – a title with political overtones, for if its adherents were in a majority they might expect to win elections. Falwell also took advantage of the modern technology of broadcasting, using the television and radio to preach to millions, and his example was followed by other revivalists. In 1978 the Virginia Beach Christian Broadcasting Network was given the use of the RCA Satcom II satellite and numerous earth stations at the cost of millions of dollars.

What is especially notable about these fundamentalist movements is that their strict adherence to the literal meaning of the Bible underlies a violent and bitter opposition to liberal and modernist Christianity, in particular the Higher Criticism of the Bible, and if anything, even more to the Darwinian theory of evolution. As a result of fundamentalist pressures bills were introduced into the legislatures of four southern states banning the teaching of evolution in schools and colleges, and a famous case was brought against a teacher, John Scopes, in Dayton, Tennessee, who had defied the ban, claiming protection under the First Amendment of the Constitution. Although he was convicted of breaking the law, the arguments of the defense so ridiculed the prosecution that many considered it a victory for liberalism. The opposition to Darwinism, however, has grown and spread in the south, and now makes a claim to scientific respectability, calling itself Creationism and arguing that Darwin's theory is at best an unproven hypothesis to which Creationism is a viable alternative.

At the present time, the requirement that secularism be maintained in politics is being deeply compromised by the increasing hold that fundamentalist Christianity has gained over government institutions – especially the United States Congress – and the extent to which the US President has encouraged and co-operated with such sects. There are to-day several fundamentalist mega-churches in the United States, some of them spreading rapidly beyond its borders. Possibly the most notable is the New Life Church which has taken over Colorado Springs as its headquarters. Its founder and present head is Pastor Ted Haggard, who is also the President of the National Association of Evangelicals which claims to include 45,000 churches and 30 million members, constituting the most influential lobbying group in the country. The church buildings and external structures of the New Life movement are modernistic and their decoration is garish; its beliefs, professed to be based upon the literal Biblical texts, are explicitly "free market"; it embraces large numbers of so-called "parachurch ministries" (Young Life, the Navigators, Compassion International, Youth Ablaze, and the like) among whose prominent ministers is Dr. James Dobson, who runs radio programs – reputed to be the most wide-ranging in the world – publishes literature and produces videos running into millions. Dr. Ted Haggard is hand in glove with President George W. Bush, who has invited him to the White House every week to meet and discuss policies with his closest advisors. Jeff Sharlet, contributing editor of Harper's Magazine, who has reported these facts, writes that "no pastor in America holds more sway over the political direction of evangelicalism than does Pastor Ted, and no church more than New Life."

Particularly alarming is the tendency of fundamentalists to accept literally the apocalyptic prophesies of the Book of Revelation and to believe that they are being fulfilled in the ensuing era. To attempt to counter or remedy actual or imminent disasters is therefore considered futile and wicked. Administrators are thus induced to disregard the urgent and ominous man-made crises by which humanity is currently threatened. Similarly disconcerting is the insistence of fundamentalists on the official requirement that public schools teach Creationism at least on a par with the theory of Evolution (and the reduction of the latter to a mere unproven hypothesis). This is generating a situation similar to, though worse than, that in the seventeenth century when the Inquisition condemned Galileo for his advocacy of Copernican heliocentrism. The modern situation is worse because the earlier dispute was not so much a conflict between religion and science, as the challenge of a new revolutionary scientific "paradigm" to an older and long established one. The Aristotelian paradigm had prevailed throughout the Ancient civilization and the Middle Ages, and had provided a philosophical basis for every aspect of civilized life and belief, from astronomy to ethics and religion, all of which seemed to be threatened by the new revolutionary concepts.[a] The position today in the United States (which has also begun to show its head in Britain) is not a legitimate dispute between scientific paradigms, but an obscurantist attempt to impose a dogmatism unsupported by evidence to the discredit of a scientific theory based upon research and empirical confirmation that has been conducted over a century and a half. In fact, fundamentalists have come to reject science and to discount the published opinions of scientists altogether, especially warnings of the consequences of global warming; so they refuse to admit the necessity to implement measures to reduce emissions of carbon dioxide and other greenhouse gases. Their influence through their representation in the United States Congress and on the President is a powerful factor in determining the refusal of that country to agree with those which have endorsed the Kyoto agreement on climate change, and obstructs action to deal with the most serious threat today to human survival.

The lengths to which this regressive movement can go is literally mind-boggling. In at least twelve states there are now initiatives to introduce legislation to restrict academic freedom by restraining professors and their assistants from maintaining that evolution is a scientific fact rather than a speculative hypothesis. The law would give students the

---

[a] As Giorgio de Santillana puts it: "It was, from the start, a conflict among the faithful themselves who disagreed about the correct approach to natural philosophy. On one side were the professors, the administrators, the representatives of ancient tradition, supported by the massive authority of Aristotle, by Greek astronomy itself. This was the house that had been built through the centuries, seemingly on a rock. On the other were the new minds who had grasped the possibility that mathematics and physics, hitherto disjoined, should effect an overwhelming conjunction to show us at last a true universe." *Reflections on Men and Ideas* (Cambridge MA and London, The MIT Press, 1968), p.64.

right to sue their teachers if they propagate beliefs that are not compatible with those of which conservative Republicans approve. Philosophy (as an academic subject) has been attacked as "leftist, Liberal totalitarianism", and in Florida the proposed Bill has been entitled "The Academic Freedom Bill of Rights", inverting the very meaning of the words.[1]

The extent to which, in violation of the First Amendment of the United States Constitution, federal politics have been tainted by ecclesiastical pressures is indicated by the altercation that has occurred over the appointment of judges to the Supreme Court. The following report appeared in the Catholic journal, *The Tablet* of 30th. April, 2005:

Despite enraged complaints, Dr. Bill Frist, the Senate's Republican majority leader, went ahead with a telecast denouncing Democrats as enemies of people of faith last week-end on 'Justice Sunday', during which Evangelicals protested the perceived liberal prejudice of the judiciary, and the Democrats' filibustering of President Bush's conservative nominations to the bench.... While the Catholic League supported Justice Sunday, Pax Christi USA decried its partisan attempt by religious conservatives to declare war on judges that don't rule in accordance to a right-wing political agenda.'

It is difficult to exaggerate the extent to which Christian fundamentalism in the United States has spiritualized politics (to use Rabbi Lionel Blue's phrase). "The result", the Rabbi writes, "would be politicized spirituality, and there is nothing more dangerous."[2]

The United States is, however, by no means the only country in which the issue of secularism has raised problems. In multi-racial countries the recent terrorist threat to western communities, which is mostly associated with Al Qaeda (a Muslim body acting professedly in defense of Islam), legislation aiming to protect the public from terrorism has frequently been interpreted as anti-Muslim and has exacerbated religious intolerance (even though not official) among the indigenous population. Although such legislation may be entirely secular in origin, if seen as antagonistic to a particular sect it can provoke, and in some cases has provoked, measures which are religiously motivated. The culprits of the September 11 atrocities in America were identified as belonging to, or being closely associated with, al Qaeda and bin Laden, who openly declare that they are waging a holy war (*Jihad*). Accordingly, they are seen as a religious movement, and anti-terrorist measures are viewed as anti-Islam (despite the misunderstanding involved, because Islam as such condemns terrorism, which the majority of Muslims disapprove. The meaning of *jihad* is "struggle" and it originally denoted internal struggle in the individual and society against evil passions and social abnormalities, rather than internecine warfare). However, the *fatwas* issued by contemporary Imams condemning terrorists as anti-Islam are discounted and ignored by those Muslims who still follow the eighteenth century Wahhabi (quasi-reformist) movement, which stigmatizes official Sunnism as heretical.

In predominantly Muslim countries for the most part secularism in politics is not observed. Turkey is an exception to this rule, owing to the reforms enforced by Kemal Ataturk after the First World War; but Iran, Indonesia and other Islamic countries, despite some recent moves in a more liberal direction, have up to the present been governed by types of autocracy and partial theocracy which are inimical to traditional democracy. And this has created problems for western democratic countries to which Muslims have emigrated along with members of other faiths, as in France where the civil government has sought to prohibit the exhibition of religious symbols in public institutions, forbidding the wearing of head-scarves by Muslim girls and of turbans by Sikhs in government schools. It also presents problems to those who, like President George W. Bush, seek to impose a western form of democracy upon Islamic countries such as Iraq, and to others who wish to see the Royal Family of Saudi Arabia give more legislative power to the common people. Yet other Islamic countries have persisted in more radical political forms, following the Shariah system of law, which western democracies regard as in many respects barbaric.

In India, the most populous of democracies, the government has from time to time become involved in the age-old, frequently violent, conflict between Hinduism and Islam, a conflict that has also infected the regime of Pakistan, and in neither of these countries is the principle of secularism scrupulously observed. Even in China, where religion is nominally outlawed by a Communistic regime, one can hardly describe the government as secular; for Communism is itself a kind of religion and its dealings with Christian and other sects cannot seriously be regarded as free from conflict with religious dogma. However, a Communistic regime is, in any case, by no means democratic in the genuine meaning of that word.

Conquest, colonialism and missionary zeal have spread Christianity and Islam throughout the world where they exist side by side with other religions. In Africa tribal beliefs have widely given way to them (although elements of paganism survive alongside other ostensible professions) and throughout the continent there are virtually as many Christian denominations as there are in Europe and America, as well as a number of home-grown varieties. Islam spread from Arabia across North Africa after the seventh century, and to east and central Africa it was brought by the Arabian slave trade. The African governments of the post-colonial era have almost all been tainted by one form or another of religious sectarianism, in many cases by more than one. The atrocities encouraged and committed by the Sudanese government against the Christian and Bantu populations of the south and west has been as much instigated by religious as by ethnic differences. On the whole, therefore, the problem of secularism in politics is one which affects governments over the entire world at the present time.

Fundamentalism is the unshakeable belief in the literal meaning of Scriptures taken to be sacred. Rationalism and logical consistency are either disregarded or held to be demonically inspired – a satanic prompting to destroy the true religious belief. Fundamentalists regard modernist secular democracy as a product of this prompting and as threatening to destroy their faith. World-wide terrorism is fuelled by this fundamentalist belief that modernism and all its products are the work of the Devil. At the same time efforts of the western nations and Israel to protect their citizens from terrorism tend to undermine civil rights that democracy is designed to preserve. Fundamentalism nullifies the authority (such as is claimed for it) of International Law. The irrationalism of fundamentalisms and their obscurantist adherence to the letter of Holy Scriptures obstructs the pursuit of knowledge, both scientific and philosophical. Its insidious penetration of government institutions in the United States, the sole remaining super-power, affects the entire world. Humanity today is faced with other problems which threaten to be terminally lethal, against the possible solutions to which fundamentalism militates; and it is itself among the most recalcitrant.

NOTES

---

[1] Cf. Jacqueline Marcus in *CommonDreams.org*, March 28. 2005.
[2] *The Tablet*, 9 July, 2005, p. 17.

5. The Decline of Contemporary Democracy

The late nineteenth and the early twentieth century conception of democratic self-government worked out by T.H Green, Bernard Bosanquet and Ernest Barker has scarcely been exemplified in more recent years either in common conceptions or in political practice. The term has been applied to very different forms of government: those in Western Europe, North America and Australasia, claiming to be liberal democracies, and others elsewhere claiming to be "people's democracies". The former refuse to recognize the latter as democracies in any sense, but rather as despotic dictatorships, not even, as they themselves have alleged, dictatorships of the proletariat. In the West it has been generally agreed that Communist regimes have no legitimate title to be styled democratic, but rather emphatically the reverse. The Soviet Union claimed to be more genuinely democratic than the liberal regimes of the west and inscribed in its constitution nominal recognition of various civil and political rights accorded to its people in terms very similar to those expressed in the constitution of the United States. But there was little, if any, evidence in practice of such recognition; rather, especially under Stalin, the government was a brutal dictatorship of the worst kind.

But what has come to be called "The Welfare State" is admitted as a democracy, albeit with the qualification "Social". It would take little (if any) adjustment of what Bosanquet called "The Philosophical Theory of the State" or what Barker described in his *Reflections on Government* to accommodate the welfare state. The concept was adopted in practice, however, by few other than the Scandinavian countries, the Netherlands, and Harold Wilson's Britain, and, with the advent of "Thatcherism" (the policies of Margaret Thatcher), the idea of social democracy which had never been popular in the United States, rather fell out of favour elsewhere as well. The doctrine of the free market and the allegedly beneficial outcome of market forces as set out by von Hayek has since become more prominent, which assigns the delivery of public welfare more to "the invisible hand" of free trade and economic competition than to the power of the people. In Britain, Tony Blair's transformation of the Labour Party into "New Labour" with his repeated call for "modernization" (unexplained and undefined) and his constant inclination when in power towards creeping privatization and policies seemingly inspired by Thatcherism have in many ways eroded the working and desired effects of the welfare state and have complicated the problems which, in any case, it had to meet.

A regrettable example of this tendency in Britain is what has happened to the National Health Service in recent years. Writing to *The Tablet* (29th, April, 2006), Dr. Elizabeth Barrett says that the government itself may not fully understand the consequences of its own policies. "Current changes," she writes,

> have the potential to put almost the whole of the NHS budget into the hands of the multinational, private sector... Two policies that will complete the privatization of the NHS are the giving of primary care contracts to multi-national private companies in order to develop 'super-surgeries,' and the policy of 'practice-based commissioning.' The commissioning budget constitutes 80 per cent of NHS spending...Once multinational companies can run general practice, they will have control of these budgets and will be able to make huge profits for shareholders as well as shaping care and services.

These policies, she avers, are driven by market ideology, not by factual evidence; the Government appears to believe that only the private sector can rescue the National Health Service, although there is no evidence that it will be better or cheaper. Similarly, Martin Lupton, a consultant obstetrician, maintains that "[o]ne of the great tragedies of this Government's approach has been to undo the magic of the working relationships within the NHS. There is a consumerist approach to medicine which makes things like parking and waiting times, which are easily measurable, appear more important than chronic illness or the standard of maternity care." Another consultant (a psychiatrist) concludes that in the free market the poor and the vulnerable would not be taken care of as well as they are at present, whatever the current deficiencies. The

NHS is a key sector of the welfare state; and much the same can be said of the effect of current government policies on education, transportation and other important social services.

To what extent this return to Adam Smith may be considered democratic is highly doubtful, especially as the outstanding writer who advocated it, von Hayek, along with other contemporary theorists (such as Schumpeter) were strongly influenced by Carl Schmitt, the prominent Nazi legal theorist and advocate of dictatorship (see ch. six below). Not all of them rejected the desirability of free voting and popular election of legislatures (although the reasons for their accepting them were the wrong ones); the doctrine relates more to the policies governments pursue than to the political form they may take, yet its effect on the principles and practice of reputedly democratic governments is profound. Reliance on market forces implies the dominance of the profit motive not only in commercial transactions, but also as a determinant of political policies, which has effects quite different from those predicted of the so-called market forces, and by no means desirable. The presumption of the theory inspiring Thatcherism is that free commercial competition will keep prices low and improve the quality of services and commodities. In practice no such results occur, because competing firms reduce quality in order to bring down the cost of production, and, as the more successful progressively eliminate those who are less able to compete, they achieve virtual monopoly, enabling them to raise prices again *ad lib*. The dominant concern of the multinational corporations is to make profit and pay high dividends to their share-holders frequently to the detriment of the services and products that they ostensibly provide. This is not the only retrograde influence; it is one that we cannot overlook, but we must also examine other developments if we are to discern the nature of modern democracy, the practices it has adopted and the forms it has taken in the latter half of the twentieth century, and those that it ought to take in the contemporary world.

Winston Churchill is reported to have said that democracy is the worst system of government, except for all the others. Current practices in the major democracies seem to bear out at least the first clause in this statement. Barker maintained with conviction that the essence of democracy was discussion at various levels from that within and (in general election campaigns) between political parties to that in the legislative assemblies. But if the aim of this discussion is the common good, its current trend seems to be less directed than it ever was towards that end. Political parties nowadays are primarily concerned with gaining power, and discussion within the party is guided more by what is likely to be popular among voters than what will serve the prosperity and welfare of the nation; politicians are all too apt to seek votes by pandering to popular tastes and prejudices and by appearing to respond to the demands of minorities whose support they perceive as significant. The final decision as to what will serve the general welfare devolves upon the mass of the voting population who are least qualified to judge, and who are most likely to vote for what they believe to be in their own individual interests. What politicians seek to serve is rather what Rousseau called "the will of all" than what he defined as "the General Will".

An outstanding example of this tendency occurred in Britain in the 1983 election when Michael Foot had become the leader of the Labour Party. He was a man of principle who refused to compromise his genuine beliefs (in particular about nuclear disarmament) in deference to popular prejudice merely with the aim of winning votes or the quest for personal advancement. He spectacularly lost the election to a Conservative leader who had overtly subordinated all other considerations to market forces, to the interests of private entrepreneurs and competition between them for higher profits, thus ushering in, for three successive parliamentary sessions, the most disastrous government Britain had suffered for decades. Its policies have privatized and closed down the coalmining industry in Britain, have destroyed the British manufacturing trade and reduced the British economy to dependence upon foreign producers both on the mainland of Europe and in the Far East. They privatized the national railways, which were, not only the first to have been developed in the world, but the best organized and most efficient, delivering them to a mélange of competing, and mutually uncooperative, companies which reduced the British rail services to a level of efficiency among the lowest in Europe. At the same time the general transport system in Britain (especially in the south-east) has become chaotic and congestion threatens to bring it to a standstill, while the ever-increasing construction of motorways threatens to obliterate much of the countryside.

Discussion within the legislature, rather than a comparison and contest between considered views of the public good, has degenerated into reciprocal competition between government and opposition in scoring debating points, frequently taking the form of mutual defamation (often merely personal). Party members are required to toe the party line and are seldom allowed to vote according to their own judgment and conscience; and there is little evidence of respect for differing opinions. Willingness among political parties to compromise is rare, and when the members of the party in power have doubts about the wisdom of any measure proposed by their government they are more likely to vote in favour of what they personally disapprove lest a possible defeat of the government should deprive the party of power.

On the positive side is the introduction by the Scandinavians of the Ombudsman, a judicial official appointed to investigate complaints against administrative actions taken in the departments of central and local government and their various agencies. The idea has spread to other countries in Europe including Great Britain. Ombudsmen are attached to each of the different departments and agencies, not excepting the Legislature itself, and the institution serves to ferret out and check malpractices, conflicts of interest, misdemeanors, and possible corruption in high places, demanding that the perpetrators be disciplined, the victims be compensated, and that malpractices be remedied and cease. It is thus a buffer against the abuse of power.

In the United States the majority of the population believes, and the politicians constantly declare, that their government is the most democratic in the world, that it insists upon the equality of persons (overlooking the practice of slavery before the American Civil War and its legacy of racism), and that its perpetual and traditional objective is the freedom of the individual. But, in fact, rhetorical respect for these characteristics is more attributable to patriotic fervor than to actual practice. Racism, indeed, seems to be on the decline and (at least in the north) is being overcome. However, whichever party is in power is in great measure financed by big business and its policies are mainly decided by the lobbying of vested interests, for the most part directly contrary to individual welfare, especially of the poorer members of society. It is questionable whether this kind of "representation" is not plutocracy rather then democracy, and whether the United States is not being surreptitiously governed by the transnational corporations.

Party conventions in America have increasingly become extravaganzas rather than serious policy discussions. Money invariably determines who is able to stand for election, especially to the Presidency, and "discussion" between parties during general elections has declined to the level of street posters and television advertisements. The so-called debates between the candidates broadcast by radio and television are rather contests in reciprocal ridicule than sincere discussions of the soundness of policies; they tend to take the form more of entertainment shows than of genuine and serious discussions of salutary government. Such developments signally fail to conform to the description of political discussion given by Barker and held to be essentially democratic; rather an ominous similarity of the American polity and personality is becoming evident to Plato's description of democracy and the democrat in the eighth book of *The Republic.*

When elected, the President strives to impose upon the legislature and the country policies that serve the vested interests that had given him financial support during the election and which he clandestinely favors. The judges of the Supreme Court, appointed by the President and approved by the Senate are almost always members of the party which the President leads and the judiciary is unduly politicized, as it is also in lower courts, where the judges are popularly elected. Such procedures hardly serve the aims envisaged by Montesquieu, whose doctrine of division of powers guided the original framers of the Constitution.

In recent years Britain has tended to move in the same direction as the United States, the Prime Minister behaving in a more presidential manner than traditionally considered proper, seeking to impose his own opinion and wishes upon Parliament rather than guiding the House of Commons, including the members of his own party within it, in the implementation of the policies decided in his Party's conventions and stated in its manifesto. Despite impassioned professions in public speeches, the intention to serve the welfare of the nation becomes progressively less apparent. With increasing frequency the will of the people, as expressed in the media, in popular demonstrations, and in the advisory opinions of scientific experts (social and physico-biological) is ignored or overruled in favour of commercial interests or alleged employment opportunities. There is evidence that recent government decisions have been made under clandestine pressure from transnational corporations contrary to the expressed wishes of large bodies of the public and the recommendations of expert associations. To a recognizable extent British politics seems to be tending, possibly because of the so-called special relation, to the adoption of American habits.

"Spin" has come to augment, if not to displace, genuine discussion and information, and the tabloid press tends to take up and emphasize what will excite and titillate the public and increase the sale of newspapers, instead of presenting, in a fair and unbiased manner, facts the knowledge of which is in the public interest. The media commonly quote details out of context in a manner that distorts the significance of what prominent persons have said, misleading public opinion, and confusing the due course of public discussion.

The decadence of the modern press with respect to political discussion and the genuine critique and comparison of policies is indicated by the way in which political reporting has shrunk in the century just passed. During the nineteenth century and the earlier decades of the twentieth, newspaper readership was predominantly the upper- class and better educated sections of the public, so political reporting and comment were informed and sober, but today newspapers (especially the tabloids) cater for all classes of the populace and the space given to sober and informed comment progressively has been reduced. The main space in contemporary newspapers is filled with reports of local and relatively trivial matters: flower-shows, local competitions (often for charity), the sexual aberrations of "celebrities", both popular and political, domestic problems, family troubles, personal details and unusual habits of well-known people. What will amuse or titillate popular emotion is preferred to more serious topics. The more important discussion of political matters tends to occupy far less space than these trivialities, and the distribution of significant information is often relegated to the inner pages or the supplements of week-end editions, and is not, even there, always predominant. The reason for this is that newspaper editors are for the most part more concerned about what will excite popular feeling, than the more weighty issues of the day. And that again is in large measure affected by the shift in public interest from government policies to more domestic and personal concerns, due to the disillusionment and boredom that many readers experience with current politics.

This growing disillusionment among the populace, especially the younger generation, is the result of the general debasement of political practice such as has been described above. People no longer believe what the politicians they elect tell them, or trust them to carry out the wishes of the electorate. So there is a growing tendency for them to refrain from voting in elections, undermining the entire conception of democratic government. In fact, universal suffrage is the indispensable foundation of democracy, without which the word itself loses its meaning. For the ancient Athenians and for Rousseau it meant the vote of all the citizens as a single constituency electing the governing body. Today the population of most nations is too great for this to be practicable, so a system of electing representatives from a number of constituencies into which the country is divided has been developed. The boundaries of these electoral districts, however, are decided by the reigning government and the practice of gerrymandering has been very prevalent.

The voting system has been corrupted even more seriously in recent times and in prospect may be so still further. In the Presidential election of 2000 in the United States, a predominantly conservative Supreme Court connived at flagrant corruption by refusing to rule on the Florida government's exclusion, on trumped up excuses (the Governor being the candidate's brother), of a large body of votes presumed to have been cast against George W. Bush; thereby disenfranchising numerous voters and ensuring the election of G.W. Bush by the Electoral College despite a majority of votes cast in the nation as a whole for his opponent. In Britain, in an attempt to counteract low turnouts at elections, the New Labour government has progressively extended postal voting, which cannot easily be protected against fraud and vote-rigging, and it has been predicted that in the near future wide-spread electronic voting via the internet may be permitted, which will make such corrupt practices easier still and yet more difficult to detect. In America voting by machine has long been practiced despite its liability to error. The cumulative result of such practices could well be total prostitution of the democratic process.

Communism having been abandoned in Russia, the new-born democracy in that country, where there has never been an established democratic tradition, seems to have withered before it has taken root. First, a Russian Mafia sprang up and flourished, creating numerous illegally prosperous millionaires. Thereafter, the Russian people seem to have preferred the somewhat peremptory rule of Vladimir Putin to any political dispute or debate, so that the Presidential election of 2004 was a foregone conclusion before it was held and Putin was swept virtually unrivalled into a fresh term by eighty percent or more of the votes. Russia is left with a predictably unstable one-man government, with no significant opposition and but few and feeble political parties, facing an uncertain future. In these circumstances, it is hardly surprising that the Kremlin is becoming more dictatorial and is placing restrictions on the media that threaten freedom of the press. The recent murders, both at home and abroad, of distinguished journalists who have been critical of the government, are events suspiciously similar to what might have occurred before the fall of the Soviets.

In all these ways "the government of the people, by the people, for the people," has degenerated into what amounts to government by vested interests under the mask of democratic procedures (where it has not been usurped clandestinely by organized crime). The transnational corporations, having come to dominate the western democracies, have, since the collapse of Soviet Communism, spread their dominion to the rest of the world beyond; and their lobbying of elected legislatures enables them to exercise an undue influence in favour of legislation to their own benefit. This process has come to be called, (despite its verbal appropriateness) somewhat misleadingly, "globalization" and is seen by many as a means of exploitation and a menace to the underdog. The "globalization" is of economic practice and interests, such as those of transnational corporations, which is detrimental, not the globalization of governmental and legal regulation, which would indeed be beneficial.

The period of colonialism during the eighteenth and nineteenth centuries had spread the ideas and influence of Western democracy beyond Europe and America to the rest of the world. But in Africa and most of Asia they were not traditional and were only partially understood. In the Muslim countries Shariah law dominated and the occasional occurrence of democratic ideas and practices at best took second place. Accordingly, when the wealth and energy of the colonial powers had been drained away by the two World Wars of the twentieth century and most of their colonies became independent, many of them, if not already taken over by despotic monarchies, became victim to military coups and tyrannical dictatorships, while others tended towards theocratic systems presided over by religious Ayatollas, at times fanatical. In many of those that profess to be democratic corrupt government functionaries have enriched themselves at the expense of the common people, while other former colonies became victims of ruthless military dictatorships (e.g., Uganda and Nigeria). In India, the largest country liberated from imperialism, resort to sectarian violence is frequently substituted for political discussion. The influence (if any) of the traditional western philosophical theory of democracy on these decolonized peoples has been minimal; and their political practices, even of the most moderate, bear little relation to it.

It seems that neither in the older more developed democracies nor in the younger decolonized polities has the traditional philosophical conception of democracy been realized, and even where it has in some recognizable degree been approached it has now declined (or is showing signs of decline) into a mere caricature.

Besides the decline in governmental practices noted above, serious questions may be raised as to the admissibility of certain current methods used by the police and law enforcement agencies, with approval, or at least connivance, of higher authorities, to extract admissions and evidence from suspected criminals: methods such as plea bargaining and offers of leniency in return for incriminating information about other suspects. Can such methods be regarded as contributing to due process of law and fair trials? It is at best very doubtful. Yet worse are the methods to which resort has been taken since the terrorist atrocities committed in New York and Washington in September of 2001 and in Madrid and in London a few years later. The British Prime Minster has said that "the rules have changed" and indeed they do seem to have, if they have not been totally disregarded and abandoned, and all on the plea of defending democracy.

Since the destruction of the World Trade Center in New York in 2001, American public opinion and politics has become obsessed with the need for security against terrorism, which is viewed as the new and most threatening enemy of democracy itself. The fear has spread in varying degrees to other countries, and the United States, now the unrivalled world super-power, has declared itself the champion of "democracy" and the implacable enemy of all international "terrorism", without distinction between terrorists and freedom fighters (as some others might regard them). This has led the American administration into military adventures, at times in disregard of world opinion and with seriously questionable results, but with the general approval at the time of the majority of the people of the United States.

First, war was waged against the Taliban in Afghanistan who were ostensibly harboring and abetting Al Qaeda and its leader Osama bin Laden, and subsequently against Iraq for alleged possession of weapons of mass destruction. Neither of these wars can be justified, either legally (in terms of International Law) or philosophically (in terms of any theory of "just war"). The pretexts for going to war was that the regimes attacked constituted an "imminent threat" to the United States: the first (Afghanistan) because the Taliban were harboring terrorists, and the second (according to Tony Blair, also an immediate threat to British interests) because Saddam Hussein possessed weapons of mass destruction and was defying the resolutions of the Security Council. But most of these pretexts proved to be groundless.

United Nations arms inspectors found no weapons of mass destruction in Iraq, whereupon President Bush asserted that they were still hidden. In the ensuing war no such weapons were deployed; he then maintained that prompt military action by the United States had prevented their use. When further searches revealed nothing, he argued that there had, nevertheless, been an imminent threat of their development; and, when no evidence of such impending development emerged, his explanation was that American action had anticipated the threat. Tony Blair, when his first pretext proved groundless, defended his decision to go to war by maintaining that regime change was essential to the safety of the region (and, presumably, of Britain) – a justification that had not been put to Parliament when he sought the approval of the House of Commons for military action, and one that overlooked the equally (or more) unacceptable regimes in other countries such as Burma and North Korea.

When the United Nations Security Council had considered what action needed to be taken in response to the alleged defiance by Saddam Hussein of its previous resolutions, it decided that lack of co-operation with its weapons inspectors would result in serious consequences – but agreement was reached only when reference to military action had been removed from the resolution. Nevertheless, the United States, disregarded the report from the inspectors that the Iraqi government was co-operating, and determined to proceed with its pre-emptive strike, which it did, with the help of Great Britain, after Tony Blair's attempt had failed to persuade the other members of the Security Council of the need for immediate action. They (more reasonably) insisted on giving the inspectors more time.

In short, these wars were illegal and unjustified, whether by International Law or by accepted theory, despite all the pious declarations in the past of democratic principles and objectives in the defense of which the military ventures were declared to have been undertaken. A policy of alleged defense of democracy pursued in breach of hitherto recognized democratic principles is oddly inconsistent and sets a precedent hardly likely to encourage and invigorate democratic practice either in the states pursuing it or elsewhere, let alone those against whom it has been directed.

The administration of George W. Bush has, in violation of the Geneva Conventions, detained for indefinite periods those captured in Afghanistan, who it is maintained are "unlawful enemy combatants," and are suspected of being (or of supporting) terrorists, in a prison-camp at the United States naval base at Guantanamo Bay in Cuba, claiming that there, being outside the territory of the United States, they are not subject to the provisions of its Constitution which protect citizens and immigrants from torture, "cruel and unusual punishments," or punishment of any kind without due process of law. The practice is flagrantly contrary to the provisions of Geneva Conventions as well, which prescribe the treatment of prisoners of war. The treatment meted out to those held at Guantanamo Bay – has been unconscionable (over and above their indeterminate detention); they have been denied legal aid, they have been held in cage-like wire enclosures, and there is reliable evidence that they have been physically and mentally tortured in the attempt to extract from them either intelligence about planned terrorist attacks on the US or confessions of committal of such acts themselves. Since the Supreme Court has subsequently ruled that Guantanamo Bay is under US jurisdiction and so subject to constitutional rules, the administration has secretly distributed many of its detainees to other centers, in Afghanistan, and elsewhere throughout the world, where their treatment is not under any surveillance and contravenes all principles of human rights or international convention.[1] In short, agreed respect for human rights and the fundamental principles of democratic practice have been flagrantly violated on the pretext of defending democracy.

The rule of law and the assumption that the accused is innocent until proved guilty by a court, have been and still are being violated in the grossest fashion. The executive has usurped powers of the judiciary and the legislature signifying total forgetfulness of James Madison's pronouncement that the concentration of powers, legislative, executive and juridical, in the same hands "may justly be pronounced the very definition of tyranny". What is still more significant is that George W. Bush was re-elected in the 2004 election, indicating the approval of such policies, so far as they were known, by the majority of Americans.

Similarly, the British government has introduced into Parliament measures enabling the Home Secretary to detain suspected terrorist without charge or trial for an indefinite period, which violate the principles of justice that have been revered since *Magna Carta* in the twelfth century, including *habeas corpus*, and illegitimately usurp the juristic function by the executive. Tony Blair, either inadvertently or deliberately, misled the House of Commons as to the reasons why it should approve of Britain's attack on Iraq, by reporting to the House that Saddam Hussein had weapons of mass destruction which could be fired within 45 minutes and were an imminent threat to the British base in Cyprus. It later transpired that the intelligence sources available to him were uncertain, that they depended on an unconfirmed report, and that the intelligence agencies regarded them with serious reservations. In fact, they proved to be entirely baseless, no weapons of mass destruction ever being found. For a Prime Minister of Great Britain so to mislead Parliament goes directly contrary to all democratic and constitutional principles previously recognized by British governments.

What is, perhaps, the most significant feature of all this illegal and unjustifiable action is that the "democracy" the United States seeks to proselytize is its own variety and it is obviously questionable whether that is the kind of benign self-government "of the people, by the people, for the people" that Lincoln envisaged, or the tradition of which earlier philosophers sought to expound. It is even more questionable whether it would be suitable to or desired by the peoples on whom it is being forcibly imposed. Such warlike and illegal policies are a sign of something even worse and more sinister. War always tends to increase the popularity and patriotic support of the executive in government. For example, when Margaret Thatcher's popular support in Britain was on the wane and her popularity was at its lowest ebb, her war against Argentina rallied patriotic feeling and restored the backing she had originally enjoyed when she won the election. Much the same, incidentally, occurred in Argentina, where the dictatorship had been engendering deep hostility until it invaded the Malvinas. Now Bush has declared war on terrorism – a new kind of war that shows no prospect of ending, against a nebulous enemy. The effect in America was to rally more popular support for the Administration and to strengthen its hand, so that it became more autocratic, more authoritarian and less democratic.

To a significant extent this trend has been strengthened by the influence in government circles (quite apart from that of "religious" fundamentalists, whose motives often seem other than spiritual, on the President) gained, over the years, by the academic followers of Leo Strauss, a school closely associated with Carl Schmitt, Hayek and Schumpeter – although, in spite of being students of Strauss, or pupils of his students, they are by no means all close followers of the master's own views; in fact, in many cases they have embraced positions that Strauss criticized adversely and are completely contrary to those he himself professed.

A number of Straussians have in various ways belittled the democratic tradition. They have extolled "conservative" virtues: for example, masculinity in men and domesticity in women; following Schmitt, they have glorified war as encouraging the manly virtues of bravery and sacrifice in the service of one's country (virtues they consider modern democracy to have weakened); and they have praised leaders in other countries who have seized dictatorial power, and have been supported by the United States for their anti-communist stance or for economic reasons.

This school (if one may so call it) has made recommendations contrary to the principle of academic freedom, such as restriction (even
dismissal) of university teachers who are left-wing or simply liberal in
their opinions, calling them "lunatic and sinister"[2] (in fact, the term "liberal" has in these days in America become as much a term of abuse as an
indication of political alignment). They also supported restrictive legislation affecting the teaching of various subjects, such as the Higher Education Act Reauthorization Bill, which set up an over-sight committee to
require study centers to serve "the information and manpower needs of
American business" and the interests of private corporations. The Bill
placed the funding for research firmly under government surveillance,
thus significantly limiting academic freedom and freedom of opinion.
Protesters against the Bill from educational organizations seeking to put
their views to the relevant congressional commission were given no
hearing, nor any opportunity to present their case.[3] The influence of the
Straussians steadily increased in government circles in recent decades
and has been consistently antidemocratic and pro-authoritarian. The
policies of the Bush Administration have been clearly directed by the
ideas published in the books of Straussians, such as *Present Dangers* by
William Kristol and Robert Kagan,[4] and Straussians have held important
federal government offices.

Many prominent Straussians have come to advocate the pursuit by
the United States of world dominance, taking advantage of its present
hegemony. They contemplate a future in which the US will establish a
pax Americana, either by force or by other methods of subjecting the international community to its will. They seek to do away with the former
professed adherence of American governments to the Monroe Doctrine
and to persuade them to pursue an imperialistic course. This imperialism
is latent behind the public statements made by the President and his
henchmen of waging "a war against evil" and ridding the world of
"rogue states", which they clearly intend to do without the approval –
rather in defiance – of the United Nations (of which most of the President's supporters disapprove and which they despise). The pretext of
regime change, that was used to justify waging war against Afghanistan
and Iraq, flies in the face of the United Nations Charter's prohibition of
intervention in the affairs of sovereign independent states, as well as all
rules of International Law against aggression.

All this is accompanied by a eulogy and commendation of war, with
the contemplation of the use of nuclear weapons if and when necessary,
in disregard of the devastation and annihilating consequences of which

scientists have assured us. Paul Wolfowitz, who worked for the government, is among those who, in company with Herman Kahn, do not regard the nuclear arsenal as a mere deterrent or as weapons of last resort.
He contemplates their use like any other weapons and assumes that a
nuclear war can be won, the cost, however unconscionable, not being
considered.

This kind of thinking accompanies an idea of a virtually holy war,
against alleged evil regimes and practices and in the pursuit of domestic
security – a notion akin to the Islamic doctrine of *Jihad*, which brings the
Straussian thinking into convergence with the fundamentalism of some
Muslims, as well as that of Pentacostalists and Evangelicals in America –
movements that have been addressed in the previous chapter – which
pose what may well be an even more serious threat to the ideals of democratic government than those discussed in this.

Attitudes such as these above described, which have not been confined to the Straussians in the Bush Administrations, hardly consort with
the tradition of democracy fostered by late nineteenth and early twentieth century thinkers, or with the concepts of self-government and liberty
entertained by the philosophers who inspired American and French
revolutionaries of the late eighteenth century. Yet they are fostered by
theorists and politicians at the opening of the twenty-first century under
the aegis of those same ideas, as the guiding principles of a crusade to
establish democracy world-wide.

Apart from the influence of government advisers who hold undemocratic theories, contemporary regimes professing to be democratic
are pursuing policies that are motivated by fear, due in great measure
to the occurrence of terrorist attacks, (a fear, as we observed, akin to
that which motivates the terrorism itself). Terrorism, however, is not
the only source of anxiety among the people and their elected rulers at
the present time. We shall discover others as we consider further the
deleterious influences eroding democracy in the new century. Government motivated by fear and concentrating almost exclusively on the desire for security is liable to lose its grip on the need of its subjects for
civil liberty and the defense of human rights, and to forget its obligation
to respect democratic practices.

NOTES

[1] Cf. the article "One Huge US Jail" by Adrian Levy and Cathy Scott Clark in the British newspaper, *The Guardian*, Weekend Section, 19th.March, 2005.

[2] Cf. Anne Norton, *Leo Strauss and the Politics of American Empire* (New Haven CT. and London, Yale University Press, 2004), p.137 and *passim*.

[3] Ibid., pp. 91f.

[4] Ibid., pp. 186ff.

6. Critique of Liberal Democracy

Criticisms of liberal democracy, of which there have been many during the last century, have focused especially on the principle of the Rule of Law. Several of them, even some that have reached repulsive and unacceptable conclusions, have had significant force and may not be dismissed out of hand by defenders of democratic liberalism, who are obliged to meet them convincingly if modern democracy is to be vindicated. Our own criticisms that have been set out in previous chapters have rather been descriptive of current trends and practices than attacks on the theoretical validity of the rule of law itself as a juridical principle; and what I now propose to examine are such attacks. The first, and most important, both for its own content and the conclusions that are drawn from it as well as for the wide influence it has exerted, is that of Carl Schmitt, the notorious jurist who at first worked as a professor in Bonn during the Weimar Republic and later became the chief juristic adviser to Adolph Hitler.[1]

The paramount principle of liberal democracy is the Rule of Law: namely, the principle that the law, properly established and enacted by the recognized institutions of government (of the people, by the people) as organized by the constitution of the polity, must apply universally and equally to all its subjects without exception. Nobody is entitled to special exemption from any of the law's provisions. Even the institutions of government, legislative, executive and judicial, and the persons who exercise these functions, are subject to law, constitutional, civil, and common.

It follows that the content of the law must be general in its application and may not affect special persons or situations only (apart from occasional exceptional circumstances of crisis requiring special remedial measures – and such exceptional measures should always be temporary and subject to periodic review).

Carl Schmitt: Schmitt argues that the rule of law is moot, because, in consequence of its generality law is bound to be indeterminate in its applications. The necessity for the law to be general in character implies that it does not delineate the particular cases to which it applies. It is thus indeterminate with respect to its precise application. If such indeterminacy were absolute, however, it would deprive the law of any application whatsoever. The indeterminacy must, therefore, be limited. Nevertheless, in its application, interpretation is called for from the judge, interpretation that is always discretionary.

Schmitt seizes upon this factor to argue, first that the judge can never be a mere mouthpiece of the law mechanically declaring what the law prescribes. To decide whether and how it applies to the present case some measure of discretion in its interpretation has to be assumed. Liberal attempts to overcome this disadvantage of the generality of law – qualifications of its prescriptions such as "in accordance with the intention of the legislator", or "the needs of commerce", or "the expressed wish of the electorate" – give no clear guidance to a judge. Nor can reference to legislative debates or historical precedents that are not themselves statutes. The judge's interpretation must accordingly be personal and in great measure arbitrary. Schmitt offers the somewhat idiosyncratic view that the only guidance available to the judge is how he considers any other judge would decide. This presupposes a general homogeneity in the thinking of the body of trained legal experts, which is not in general to be met with. Schmitt, however, came to identify it with ethnic homogeneity, what he called *Volksgebundenheit* that, in due course, was invoked to justify the ruthless elimination of non-Arian elements in the German population and judiciary undertaken by the National Socialist dictatorship.

The final conclusion reached by Schmitt of the necessity and desirability of dictatorship as the natural successor to democracy was in part suggested to him by the military dictatorship to which Germany was subject towards the end of the First World War, and partly due to his aversion to the difficulties and crises experienced during the subsequent Weimar Republic. But the trend of his thought is detectable even in his early pre-war writings dating back to 1912.

The next phase of Schmitt's development consists, to begin with, in an attack on political realists who contend that the normative claim of law and legal argument are nothing but cloaks to cover what is really a conflict between rival social and political interests. Schmitt rejects this position emphatically, arguing that law is essentially normative: it states what *ought to be*, whereas socio-political struggles are merely factual, relating to power rivalries. There can be no transition from the merely factual sphere of power-politics to the sphere of the "ought". This argument conforms to that of the philosophers, Hume and Kant, who maintain that "ought" can never be derived from "is"; and it is also closely akin to Hans Kelsen's theory of positive law, in which he asserts that law is purely normative and consists of series of interdependent norms, each derivable from a prior norm and all derivative from a basic norm distinguishable only by the fact that it comes first.

Schmitt, however, parts company with Kelsen (they were colleagues at the University of Bonn during the Weimar period) – in fact, he argued against his position as strenuously as he did against the political realists – and with some justice, for Kelsen's view of law as a norm loses its main force if the norm is deprived of content – if all that distinguishes the basic norm is its priority. (The doctrine is similar to Kant's ethical theory which deprives the good will of content by defining it as the will to act solely from the motive to act rightly, providing no criterion of what is morally right). Schmitt, on the other hand, seeks to find a way to reconcile law and politics, by asserting that the state converts the law into practicality. In the course of this transition, however, the law loses its normative character and becomes the instrument of sheer power. The law is given factual effect only by a sovereign act. Hence the normative character of law is, as it were, absorbed into power by a political act unconstrained by any norm (since sovereignty is subject to no higher authority). This is how Schmitt resolves the problem of legal indeterminacy.

The next step is to trace back this conversion of law into power to the *Urzustand* (the original situation) in which law is the dictate of the absolute monarch. Schmitt approaches the process of transition through a discussion of the concession made by liberal theorists in the case of crisis situations, which are held to warrant special administrative powers to meet an exceptional state of affairs. Against the objections of the traditional German jurists, who opposed the claim to unlimited political power by the generals who ruled Germany in the final stages of

World War I, Schmitt defended the generals' claim.[a] But his defense was not simply based on the necessity imposed by the emergency; it followed from his contention that effective law is inevitably tainted by the element of power. The doctrine legitimizing the suspension of legal regulation during a state of emergency, insofar as that involves the violation of, and presupposes a separation of legislative from executive functions in normal times, depends (he contends) on a false premise. The inevitable dependence of the law on discretionary executive decision stems, Schmitt maintains, from the *Urzustand* and cannot be overcome in any circumstances. He proceeds to argue that the impossibility of overcoming the fusion of legal and executive discretion is the ever-present underpinning of dictatorship. As dictatorship is thus more in keeping with the ubiquitous nature of legislative decision, it is preferable and more appropriate to the function of government than liberal democracy, which is founded on a misconception. The liberal notion of the rule of law is, therefore, no more than a sop to justify (and disguise) the constant and inevitable power struggle between political parties.

Schmitt's main critique of contemporary parliamentarism was written in three works during the Weimar period: *Die geistesgeschichtliche Lage des heutigen Parlamentarismus* (translated as *The Crisis of Parliamentary Democracy*), *Verfassungslehre* (*Constitutional Theory*), and *Der Hüter der Verfassung* (*The Guardian of the Constitution*). They are scholarly works appreciative, though sternly critical, of the main political theory writers of the eighteenth and nineteenth centuries. But his critique is, perhaps, most remarkable for the new and special meanings that he gives to the terms "politics" "parliamentarism", "democracy", and "representative". He begins with a description of the nineteenth century conception of parliamentary deliberation which (rather surprisingly) has much in common with Ernest Barker's analysis of democratic procedures. Schmitt asserts that it consisted essentially of rational discussion among parliamentarians who were open to persuasion and sought the best and most convincing arguments, so that they might from time to time find themselves in agreement with those whom they had previously opposed. He attributes the possibility of parliamentary debates approximating to this ideal to the fact that the members of legislative assemblies were drawn from the wealthier and better educated classes among whom could be found (as he puts it) "particles of reason that are strewn unequally among human beings."[2] Nowadays, however, as a result of the extension of the suffrage to the mass of the population, parliamentarians represent

---

[a] Schmitt worked for the military dictatorship in 1917-18.

great popular movements (such as Marxism and Democratic Socialism), factions seeking power, not a "common good" of the whole, which the nineteenth century thinkers, as Schmitt would say, imagined. Members of parliament can no longer take an unbiased view of affairs, but seek to advance the cause of one or another ideology by means of slanted propaganda.

Unlike Barker, Schmitt does not believe that the mass of the people can participate in discussion; they can only answer Yes or No to straightforward questions put to them by a higher authority; at most, they can vote, and accept or reject a general decision of a governing body. He is thus eventually led to recommend, as the most appropriate political form, a plebiscital dictatorship.

Schmitt rightly saw that the civil rights on which liberal democrats insist are all closely connected with the idea of free, rational, parliamentary debate; but he holds that this whole conception of democracy overlooks (or is unaware of) what he calls "the concept of the political" and in consequence has now become outdated – or indeed was never really valid. His concept of politics is that it is always power-politics, always adversarial – a conflict between hostile camps that implicitly seek each to eliminate its opponent. The implication of political activity (tacit or open) is always a friend/foe relationship with the intention of killing the foe (Schmitt's judgment of human nature is akin to Oswald Spengler's: that man is a beast of prey). Liberal parliamentarism is thus anti-political and anachronistic and never really actual. Democratic politics, as Schmitt understands it, on the other hand, *is* political, so liberal parliamentarism and democracy are in fact antithetical.

The reason for this is that democracy (as the term implies) seeks to identify the people with the government (it seeks to be *self*-government) and such identity can be brought about in more ways than one. It can be achieved by Communism or Fascism just as well as, or possibly even better than, by democratic practice. Do not Communist regimes claim to be people's democracies? It is because these movements see themselves as vitally opposed to their rivals, and engage in a political struggle that is internecine that they are truly political, and so far as the conflict takes place in a popularly elected legislature democracy is genuinely political. This is what accounts for the deterioration of parliamentary debate from the nineteenth century ideal of rational discussion. It has nowadays descended to mutual vilification by the contending parties and defamatory attacks upon their members.

Representation, for Schmitt, also takes on a peculiar new meaning. It is not the presentation by an elected person of the viewpoint and wishes of his or her constituents so much as the manifestation in a charismatic political leader of the purposes and aspirations of the people he represents, which they are unable to express or achieve unaided. It is, in effect, leadership (*Fhürerschaft*). In short, Schmitt's thinking gravitates constantly towards what he finally embraced: National Socialism.

As already indicated, Schmitt did not really believe that the ideal of parliamentary discussion was ever actual, and he believed that if it ever was it would have been extinguished by left-wing political developments of the time in which he was writing, because these movements have had the effect of homogenizing the electorate and persuading the masses that they can take meaningful part in the political conflict, whereas all they can really do is answer Yes or No to questions put to them from the political élite who are their effective rulers. The traditional humility of the less educated mass of the people in respect to their superiors, who alone have the necessary political competence, is thus lost. The main targets of Schmitt's attack are political parties supporting labour unions, social welfare, and communism, which he believed were the root source of the troubles experienced by the Weimar Republic.

As we have already observed, the liberal reliance on the rule of law involves general submission to the law of the Constitution. The Constitution, however, originates from a legislative act consequent upon the decision of a constituent assembly. Schmitt has maintained that every law is enacted by a sheer act of will unrestrained by any extraneously imposed legal norm, and that this is implicit in the liberal admission of the legislative competence of parliament. It will, of necessity, apply even more strongly to the constitution itself, which originally issues from the unfettered decision of a constituent assembly and is confirmed by the act of the constituted legislature. It is thus established by a pure act of will. The constitution therefore originates in an arbitrary act of the constituent assembly, and can be amended by a similar act of the legislature (usually with an especially decreed enhanced majority). On these grounds, Schmitt argues, Constitutional Law is as little normative as any other, and the liberally acclaimed rule of law is at best a cover for the ubiquitous power politics that prevails not only within the state, but between the state and its actual or potential enemies.

This is so because the constituting power is the sovereign nation and is derivative originally from the *Urzustand*. Moreover, the sovereignty of the nation (historically originating as embodied in an absolute

Monarchy) is essentially what defends it from potential enemies and thus represents *par excellence* the concept of the political. The somewhat thinly veiled implication is that the constitution itself is an implicit threat to foreign nations – a potential act of war. So far as politics within the state is concerned, however, Schmitt contends that the participation of the nation, inasmuch as that is constituted by the people, is minimal, as they are capable only of answering simple questions with Yes or No. So the national will can be expressed in detail only by the political élite who pose the question.

The final result of the development of liberal parliamentarism, according to Schmitt, is the "total state". The account he gives of this development is shot through and through by application of his "concept of the political" – various patterns of conflict between rival elements. The main burden of his argument is that the liberal democratic state of the nineteenth century as it extended the franchise to the lower classes of the people in the following century inevitably grew into a purely decisionist executive administration, essentially interventionist, regulating those activities that in the previous period had been confined to "society", and from interference with which the government had refrained. Early liberal democracy was essentially non-interventionist, and so was able to remain genuinely political. As it was controlled by the aristocratic and educated classes of the population it retained elements of former monarchical absolutism which enabled it to resist liberal pressures to enfranchise the working class. It was this latent conflict that gave nineteenth century liberal democracy an ambivalent character: on the one hand, its radical tendencies made it "antipolitical"; on the other, the monarchical relics still implicit in it enabled it to remain executively "political".

According to Schmitt, modern liberalism released popular social forces fighting for social justice which brought parliament, seeking to introduce reform, into conflict with the wealthy economic élite who controlled the executive. Popular movements progressively came to monopolize parliament generating more and more interventionism on the part of the government until the distinction between legislature and executive became blurred. Government was overwhelmed by its efforts to deal with economic and social problems, becoming more and more decisionist, so that such liberal restraints as "the rule of law", became irrelevant and classical liberal ideas and practices were simply anachronistic.

The efforts of the state to cope with economic problems led to conflict between rival economic interests which, Schmitt perspicaciously contends, spilt over into the international sphere and provoked actual warfare. As the twentieth century advanced, hope increased that conflict could be eliminated by technology which could solve economic problems by reducing scarcities. It then became imperative that governments made technology their main concern as technical matters increasingly came to dominate the friend/enemy relations pervading politics. These manifested themselves in economic competition in the domestic sphere and in national autarchic rivalries in the international arena. In particular, government finds it essential to concern itself with the developing technology of the mass media: radio, film, and printed news dissemination (today we should add television), which offered the unprecedented prospect of mass persuasion and manipulation of public opinion. Consequently all thought of non-intervention in the realm of communication is abandoned.

What began as liberal democracy has thus, by its very nature, developed into the total state in which the executive predominates, and for which, Schmitt considered, an authoritarian form of government was best equipped to deal with economic and technical demands. Schmitt ascribes the emergence of the total state to the increased predominance in the legislature of parties, Social Democratic, Marxist, Conservative, etc., which themselves had become total, embracing the provision of facilities for education, sport, and leisure activities for their members. Their representatives in parliament form antagonistic blocs, uninterested in and incapable of rational discussion. They follow the general character of the total state and themselves become totalitarian. Schmitt deplores what he calls "the societalization of the state", and declares that it is foreign to the German tradition and is the product of "western" influences. He considers the tendency of the total state towards executive totalitarianism, however, to be its positive feature. Interventionism and totalitarianism turn out to be complementary aspects of the same political process, and the latter is what recommends itself to Schmitt as the sole efficient alternative form of modern government. The logical conclusion is, for him, National Socialism and his adherence to the Nazi party was its natural consequence.

The period from 1933 to 1945 is the most prolific of Schmitt's career and also the most infamous for its crude anti-semitism and baseless vilification of the Jews. His diatribes cannot be passed off as mere time-serving concessions to the Party leadership, for the seeds of these outbursts can be traced back to his earliest writings as far as 1912 when he assigned the possibility of legal determinacy to the existence of a homogeneous judiciary, the premonition of his later recommendation of ethnic homogeneity and *Volksgebundenheit* in the German judiciary.

During his Nazi alignment, Schmitt wrote extensively on international law and the effect upon it of indeterminism. Much of his criticism is perspicacious and accurate and coincides with what other critics, roughly contemporary, who were advocates of liberal democracy, also recognized. Schmitt perceived that the League of Nations provided no more than a disguise for power politics, which Georg Schwarzenberger some years later demonstrated convincingly. Schmitt also discerned that such power politics was consequent upon the sovereign claims of independent national states, a fact emphasized by George Keeton at much the same time. These aspects of his critique deserve careful consideration by current theorists of international law. But Schmitt complicates his penetration in these respects with analyses and interpretations which either tacitly presuppose much that he is disposed to reject, or contradict the strictures he constantly offers against liberal normativism, or both; so he is able to use the conflicting elements of his theorizing to justify the twists and turns of Nazi foreign ventures, as when Hitler first signed a treaty with France and Britain undertaking not to occupy more of Czechoslovakia than the Sudetenland, peopled by Germans, along the western border (which happened to be the most strategically defensible), then violated it by overrunning the whole of the country; and when he made a non-aggression pact with Stalin and later attacked the Soviet Union.

Schmitt inveighs against the mutual bellicosity of independent national states, yet supports the Nazi claim to reoccupy the Saar and Rhineland on the grounds of German sovereignty and national interest. The alternative he recommends to international enmities is a plurality of ethnically homogeneous peoples living side by side, each in its own *Grossraum* (large space), under the dominance (*Reich*) of the most influential. He condemns any attempts at intervention in the internal affairs of one by another (a conception accepting, in effect, the very notion of the equal status of sovereign states attested by current International Law, which he derides as mythical and false); yet he finds ways and principles by which to justify Nazi aggression in all directions conducted by Hitler.

Our reflections on Schmitt's doctrine must emphasize three considerations: first, that its direct outcome is execrable and utterly repulsive; second, that it nevertheless draws attention to defects in the concept of liberal democracy that the advocates of liberalism cannot afford to overlook or dismiss out of hand; third, that its influence on other writers and in other countries has been far from negligible and can but have serious consequences. The first of these topics needs no further comment, as any right-minded person cognizant of the destruction, death, genocide and widespread mayhem occasioned by Hitler's policies and the Second World War that they initiated can but agree that it must obviously be true. The second topic deserves careful investigation and discussion, but in order that the historical sequence should not be broken, we shall do well to continue by devoting the next section to another important writer whom Schmitt has influenced.

Joseph A. Schumpeter: Schumpeter was a colleague of Schmitt's in Bonn during the 1920s. They knew each other personally and each was acquainted with the other's work. They took part in discussions on liberal parliamentarism and there is evidence from Schmitt's correspondence that he admired many of Schumpeter's ideas, which, in a number of respects were closely similar to his (Schmitt's) own. Schumpeter was on the editorial board of a learned journal that published some of Schmitt's more important papers and records indicate that Schumpeter was deputed to encourage Schmitt to pursue his work on the Concept of the Political, of which in correspondence Schumpeter expressed admiration. In his definitive work on that topic, Schmitt cites with approval Schumpeter's pronouncements on imperialism. In fact, he makes frequent references to Schumpeter's writings, with which he was clearly well acquainted. The similarities and near coincidences in the expressed views of the two writers are numerous and such differences between them as are evident can for the most part be attributed to the fact that Schumpeter was an economist, whereas Schmitt was a jurist, by training.

Schumpeter's central contention is that the driving force of modern economic and political development is the enterprise and energy of the capitalist entrepreneur, whose contribution is obfuscated and disowned as the result of the inevitable evolution of liberal democratic society into an overburdened bureaucratic state socialist system. The creative entrepreneur, Schumpeter declares, can engage in decisive and progressive economic activity in unforeseeable circumstances, his preparedness to take risks seeming sometimes to be irrational. At the same time, Schumpeter holds, the developed methods of modern capitalism (as Max Weber had maintained) are the main source of the rationalistic outlook and procedures of contemporary democracy. Capitalist business methods become more and more systematic and disciplined – based on strict calculation, accurate book-keeping, and scientific machine technology.

Concurrently the bourgeoisie, from among whom the entrepreneurs are drawn, decline as a class. They not only educate their enemies (the working class), says Schumpeter, but allow themselves to be educated by them. Accordingly, they lose faith in their own system and put up weak, if any, resistance against attack, always being ready to compromise. The socio-political effect is that class privileges are annulled and social status leveled, resulting finally in a systematized state socialism with an economy dominated by a minimum of huge bureaucratically organized firms whose leadership is a body of expert technicians and highly trained specialists. Thus the creative enterprise of the entrepreneur is eliminated and replaced by calculated planning issuing in monotonous routine.

Schumpeter deplores this outcome and commends in its stead the encouragement of the entrepreneur, whom he sees as a courageous and charismatic figure able to get things done even at the cost of taking risks that the calculating planner would shun. The source of economic growth, he believes, is not the fluctuation of supply and demand but a process that he calls creative destruction: new methods of production constantly being developed which destroy the old by making them obsolete and inefficient in comparison. The new methods are the inventions and innovations introduced by the creative activity of entrepreneurs who compose the economic élite. This economic élite plays the part in Schumpeter's doctrine that the political élite plays in Schmitt's.

While this is perhaps the most significant convergence between the thinking of the two writers, there are a great number of others. They both evince respect for Max Weber and begin from appreciation of some of his ideas, while they diverge from others. They both envisage (in some ways invent) an ideal liberal past, which they lament, but which cannot be recovered because of the irreversible trends of contemporary social and economic development. Schmitt ascribes the success of nineteenth century parliamentary government to the fact that representatives were drawn exclusively from the aristocratic and wealthy classes, and so does Schumpeter. Both ascribe political decisions to irrational willing and maintain that government is dominated by the executive. As Schmitt is dismissive of contemporary popular self-government, so is Schumpeter of economic democracy. Schumpeter defends the "irrational" capitalist entrepreneur willing to risk the unknown, as Schmitt defends dictatorial leadership against law abiding liberal parliamentarism. Both criticize representative democracy as anachronistic and deplore the decline of reasonable political debate into strife between mass parties appealing to irrational prejudices, and the displacement of responsible parliamentary representation by members obedient to the party whips, conforming to the party line at the bidding of party bosses who appeal to the worst motives. Both writers attribute these characteristics to the quest for equality and the growth of mass political parties. Like Schmitt, Schumpeter sees increasing socialism as destructive of democracy (admitting, however, that socialism is a workable system), and its elimination of the entrepreneur as leaving his function open to be filled by a political dictator able to maintain economic order and discipline in the workplace. They both admit the need for such dictatorship to use the technology of modern communication to manipulate public opinion in a plebicitary regime.

Lamenting the growth of all-inclusive democracy, Schumpeter echoes Schmitt in admitting its compatibility with racial and ethnic homogeneity, although he stops short of recommending ethnic cleansing. Schumpeter's description of the inevitable transition of liberal democracy into state socialism, as the effect of increasing government intervention and regulation in a capitalist economy, parallels Schmitt's exposition of the process of development of the total state.

There are, of course, also significant differences in the conclusions reached by the two thinkers. But the arguments of Schumpeter's major work, *Capitalism, Socialism and Democracy*, seem definitely to have been shaped by his debates with Schmitt when they were colleagues in Bonn; and although there is no admission in the book of any debt to Schmitt, that may well be for no better reason that in the 1940s in America, where Schumpeter was then teaching at Harvard, to admit debts to Schmitt would have meant academic suicide. The same consideration may have induced Schumpeter to introduce into his analysis certain concessions to modern democratic aspirations, which are partial departures from his central thesis, such as free competition between aspiring leaders for the vote of the electorate, despite his admission of manipulation by the élite of public opinion through the media. At the same time, Schumpeter exercised significant and widespread influence upon American political science as his avoidance of a totalitarian fascist conclusion helped to make many of Schmitt's ideas seem palatable to American thinkers, who were themselves critical of contemporary democratic practices.

Vilfredo Pareto: An Italian writer, much admired by Schumpeter, is Vilfredo Pareto. Schumpeter borrowed several of Pareto's ideas and used them to support his comparatively rare differences with Schmitt, with whose position, however, Pareto's had a not inconsiderable overlap. Pareto, like these two authors, emphasized the virtues of a ruling élite and expressed strong distrust of popular decision-making. The majority of people, he held, were habitually irrational, so that egalitarian democracy appeared to him to be pure absurdity. Popular self-government he regarded as a contradiction in terms. He was entirely committed to market capitalism (a characteristic in common with Friedrich Hayek whom we shall consider shortly).

Although there is much agreement between Pareto and Schmitt (who also expressed admiration for him), Pareto insists on what he describes as a circulation of élites – not contemplated by Schmitt – for the maintenance of a reliably capable group of leaders. He points out that the purposes of the social group determine the kind of capability and expertise desirable in its leaders, which is the source of their privileged predominance. And as a specialized élite tends to rigidify and deteriorate, it needs to be periodically replaced by others risen from the lower ranks of society. Political systems that hinder such circulation become unstable, while those which provide means to a smooth transition for such interchange of élites promote repeated regeneration of leadership and are less prone to disorder and revolt.

These authors (in particular Pareto and Schumpeter) viewed traditional political theories simply as bad philosophy and the notion of a common good mere rubbish. Democratic slogans and professions on the part of aspiring leaders they considered simply to be myths used by the members of élites seeking political power.

Pareto's writing paved the way to Mussolini's Fascism, much as Schmitt's provided Hitler with a juristic and politico-theoretical basis for Nazism, indicating how easily right-wing criticism of democracy can lead down a slippery slope into totalitarianism, racist persecution and tyranny of the most execrable nature. And there are other writers in whose work echoes may be discerned of doctrines inspired by Schmitt and Schumpeter. Ortega-y-Gasset was a somewhat earlier contemporary, who in his book *The Revolt of the Masses* is nostalgic for the rule of the élite and rather more than suspicious of mass demands for equality and power; and Spain was the third country to suffer autocratic oppression: that of Franco and the Fallange.

Friedrich A. von Hayek: Von Hayek was the high priest of free market conservatism, which is not usually associated with Carl Schmitt; yet Hayek's open acknowledgement of his debt to Schmitt is generally overlooked. Hayek alleged that the rise of the welfare state, typically accompanied by state interventionism was "the road to serfdom". The first line of Hayek's argument is taken directly from Schmitt: that demands for equality and social justice result in intervention by the state in economic relationships that sets it on a course of development leading to socialism and ultimately to authoritarian rule – according to Hayek, to serfdom. This is the course taken by the welfare state which should, therefore, be avoided at all costs. The only tolerable alternative, Hayek believed, was to allow market forces free rein unhampered by legislation. This conclusion is not as far from Schmitt's as has generally been supposed by those (like Margaret Thatcher) who regard democratic freedom as the obverse of *laissez faire* economics, and who need to consider more carefully the implications of Hayek's dependence on Schmitt's reasoning.

Schmitt had agitated (in the late 1920s and early 1930s) against the Weimar Republic's pioneering attempts to establish a social welfare state that involved intervention by government in the social and economic relationship of the working and employing classes. Such interventionism, Schmitt argued, undermined the rule of law that required legal generality and restraint from discrimination between the subjects to which the law applied. Intervention permitted by social welfare legislation allowed the state to issue decrees in favour of special interests (what he designated "revolutionary violence").

The remedy for this, he maintained, was not a return to nineteenth century liberalism, any attempt at which he considered futile, but the replacement of the emerging "quantitative" total state by a "qualitative" total state that would be compatible with the privileged status of private capital (*Bildung und Besitz*). It was this type of state that enabled Hitler to aspire to national autarchy. Hayek accepted Schmitt's assessment of the interventionist social welfare state, but proposed as its antidote what Schmitt had rejected.

With the Nazi atrocities fresh in everybody's mind after World War II, right-wing politics and economics were shunned and left-wing social welfare was in demand, with its nationalization of health care, transport, and public services. It was just at this time that Hayek published *The Road to Serfdom*, in which he argued that the move to social welfare threatened the rule of law. His supporting arguments are lifted, lock, stock and barrel, from Schmitt – except that he fails to notice that Schmitt used his references to the nineteenth century liberal ideal simply as a convenient prop to his criticism of Weimar socialization, rejecting it as a practical alternative.

Quoting Schmitt explicitly, Hayek contends that the state's intervention in the economy leads to a "total state" involving arbitrary (willful) legislative acts that eliminate the distinction between the legislative and executive functions of government (Schmitt's doctrine). Accordingly, the interventionist state corresponds, in its general tendency and legal character, to the plebiscitary dictatorship described by Schmitt, in which the people simply endorse the will of the executive-legislature. So the post-war social democratic trend, Hayek argues, is leading inevitably to the very demonic type of authoritarianism that the victorious powers had just vanquished. He resorts, however, to a return to the *laissez faire* liberalism current prior to World War I, which Schmitt considered anachronistic. Despite his aversion to Schmitt's support and advocacy of Nazism, Hayek contrasts Schmitt's earlier writings with those of the Nazi period, praising the former as among the most perceptive and learned.

Following Schmitt's early arguments, Hayek makes the generality of the law central to the liberal ideal; although he never succeeds in defining it in precise terms, but leaves the concept obscured by ambiguities, and he is himself uncertain of its exact implications. Despite his antagonism (following Schmitt) to the "decisionist" procedures of the welfare state, his own recommendations are not free of similar decisionist elements, largely due to his borrowings from Schmitt. In his later works. Hayek openly endorses Schmitt's criticism of what he calls "the pluralist party state" and himself presents a critique that echoes Schmitt in every detail averring that the social democratic legislature becomes an arena for bargaining between interested parties rather than a chamber for genuine deliberation over the common welfare. The powers assumed by the legislature obscure its proper function and reduce it to a cockpit of dispute between special interests (trades unions, professional bodies, capitalist institutions, etc.), ultimately depriving it of real legislative power. The outcome is a "fusion of state and society" that generates a "quantitative total state". The remedy Hayek proposes is a legislature restricted to enacting general laws and held to this function by a surveillant Upper House with few members and relieved, as far as possible, of the need for frequent re-election. The activities of such a body, he admits, are bound to be discretionary. This implicit convergence with Schmitt's dictatorial conclusion, according to which the only alternative to the pluralistic party state is an authoritarian regime liberating private capital from interference, Hayek finds attractive because it seems to him to be a return to a political system dominated by the propertied and educated classes (a system viewed by Schmitt with equal nostalgia), to whom he believed the welfare state to be a menace.

Hayek earned for himself the highest academic eminence. He taught in Austria at Vienna, in England at London, in America at Chicago and in Germany at Freiburg. He shared the Nobel Prize for economics with Gunnar Myrdal and his influence both in Europe and America was immense, especially in the United States at the time, during the Cold War, when McCarthyism was most virulent. In England, the impression he made was in great measure responsible for Margaret Thatcher's policies, which had reverberations throughout Europe. In America, it served to disseminate the latent influence of Schmitt along with the more evident influence of Schumpeter among the more important writers on political theory. Although Hayek increased the tendencies to concentrate upon market forces, giving scope to the effects of the profit motive in economic transactions, whereas Schmitt inclined thinkers more in the direction of illiberal conservatism, these trends overlapped sufficiently to reinforce each other, and they were not inconsiderable in the impression they made on the Straussians of whom we have already spoken.

Hans Morgenthau: Strauss was well acquainted with Schmitt's work and had criticized some of his ideas in pre-war days. Likewise, Hans Morgenthau had been impressed as a graduate student by Schmitt's conception of the political and had criticized it in his doctoral dissertation. It is clear that the criticism caught Schmitt's eye, for in his 1932 revision of the doctrine he modified it in the direction Morgenthau had indicated. In fact, Morgenthau claimed that Schmitt had written him a complimentary letter after the dissertation had been published, and later alleged that Schmitt had actually plagiarized it without acknowledgement.

Morgenthau's criticism, although at times it seems to be somewhat hair-splitting and logic-chopping, points out that Schmitt's use of the friend/enemy relationship does not conform to common usage which applies it to subjects that Schmitt seeks to exclude from the political sphere. In particular, Schmitt insists that morality is always irrelevant in the political context, while Morgenthau is able to argue convincingly that this does not follow logically from what is alleged to be the concept of the political. This, however, is a purely theoretical point and only in Morgenthau's early writings is it prominent. In his later work there are a number of issues on which he is in effect in agreement with Schmitt, although his reasons are not the same. Where Schmitt argues that morality and politics are mutually incompatible and that liberal attempts to apply moral criteria to political action are fraudulent and farcical, Morgenthau admits that liberals often mistakenly confuse political matters with economic and moral considerations in their attempts to justify inconsistent and immoral policies, as when they seek to excuse military ventures on the grounds that they are undertaken in the interests of the party attacked (liberating people from tyranny, or correcting unfair economic restrictions) while at the same time they condemn as aggression the warlike assaults of other governments. Both writers diagnose the evils and errors endemic in international relations correctly, but they react in opposite ways. Morgenthau wishes to limit such liberal self-deception by reforming the methods of international politics so as to limit, as far as possible, their costly effects; unfortunately he sees few if any ways of doing so. Schmitt, on the contrary, merely deprecates the hypocrisy of the liberal pretences to legitimize power politics while he considers the violence of its process appropriate to the rule of unavoidable dictatorship.

Morgenthau is a political realist, so he can see the ills to which international relations between sovereign nations give rise, and his diagnoses in many ways coincide with Schmitt's. Both see the Monroe Doctrine as means at once to facilitate United States' imperialism in Latin America and to ward off interference by the European powers. Both realize that the failure of the League of Nations and the troubles of the interwar period were due to the utopian liberalism of President Wilson in the face of the limitations and inadequacies of International Law. But again Schmitt simply dismisses International Law as a useless and impossible attempt to submit international affairs to legal norms, while Morgenthau seeks to discover the causes of its failings in the hope (unfulfilled) of remedying them.

Morgenthau was a Jewish refugee from Germany after 1933. First he taught in Geneva, until the persecution of German students caused him to resign. Then he moved to Madrid, but was again driven out by Franco's victory over the republican resistance. In America he became one of the outstanding political theorists of the post-war period and exercised powerful influence. But it is not clear how far those who admired and followed his theorizing realized his differences from Schmitt rather than recognizing the similarity of their arguments. There has been a revival of interest in Schmitt in America in recent years, disconcertingly apologetic: the "postmodernist" school welcoming his criticism of liberalism seemingly without appreciating the disastrous conclusions to which it leads. In recent decades (as we observed earlier) the term "liberal" has in many quarters become as much a term of abuse as a designation of political orientation.

Benjamin R. Barber: Not all critics of modern democracy begin from the indeterminacy of the law, or the menace of excessive governmental power in the social welfare state. One, at least, is more troubled by the current conception of liberty that is entertained by professed Liberals, many, if not most, of whom are strictly conservative rather than liberal in their political alignments. The writer who takes his starting point from this issue is Benjamin Barber.

Irrespective of the degeneration and perversion of democracy that was described in former chapters, modern liberal democracy has been criticized as the contemporary development from the uncompromising individualism of early political philosophy, such as that of Hobbes, Locke and the Enlightenment, in consequence of which the prevailing motive of modern liberalism is an inveterate opposition between government as such and the inalienable rights of the individual to his or her undisturbed personal liberty free from all interference. Such liberty is purely negative – a freedom *from* incursion, rather than a freedom *to* co-operate with one's fellow citizens in obtaining common benefits. "Liberal" theorists (as well as practitioners) all seek to base their thinking on the notion of an original, isolated, non-social (or even anti-social) individual, as well as an "objective" criterion of truth established independently of the political process. All this has been attributed to the influence, in the seventeenth century and later, of Newtonian (atomistic and mechanistic) science.

Benjamin Barber is the author who has set out this critique and it is in many respects correct.[a] The fact that, in the presumed State of Nature, when disputes or conflicts arose between individuals each man would be judge in his own case led Locke and others who have thought in these terms to admit the inevitability of some sort of social interaction that requires enforced regulation of human behavior the aim of which should be, they thought, to preserve as far as possible, the individual's "natural rights" to freedom from interference. Political power is then viewed "realistically" as a necessary evil, and the result is a concept of limited government restricted to the prevention of encroachment upon the freedom of the subject, a limitation which has to be ensured by constant vigilance on the part of the subject and established by pitting governmental functions one against another.

---

[a] Cf. Benjamin R. Barber, *Strong Democracy* (Berkeley, Los Angeles, London, University of California Press, 1984, 2003). Compare my presentation of a similar argument in *Apocalypse and Paradigm* (Westport CT., Praeger Press, 2000).

Benjamin Barber inveighs against this type of "liberalism" and its assumption of a "truth" antecedent to political order and practice – a pre-existent state of nature entailing inherent, inalienable rights. He criticizes the attendant form of what he calls "Thin Democracy", and seeks to substitute for it what he terms "Strong Democracy" based on the willing co-operation of citizens in non-governmental associations seeking commonly desired social benefits. He also uses the phrase "participatory democracy" to designate this form of polity. Others, mostly Trotskyites, have used the phrase to designate the practice of submitting every political issue to discussion by the entire popular constituency until unanimous agreement is reached. Such procedure, however, almost invariably leads to endless wrangling, and seldom concludes with general agreement, let alone unanimity. To adopt it generally would almost inevitably lead to paralysis of the political process.

What Barber is describing, however, is more what Ernest Barker identified as Civil Society in distinction from Political Order. Such civil society is concurrent and, in the main, co-extensive with the established political organization and in actual fact is dependent upon it for its stability and success; because the activities of civil associations cannot be secure, nor can they be wholly free from partisanship with its incurable conflict and dispute, unless protected and regulated by the law as it is interpreted and applied by the courts; and so far as these local citizens' councils succeed, their agreed decisions cannot be reliably implemented, unless they can be statutorily enacted.

Barber wishes to substitute the "participatory" process for representative government, maintaining that representation deprives the individual citizen of his or her responsibility for the values and principles on which political decisions and actions are based. Voting for a representative leaves such matters to others to discern (a presumed élite): as Rousseau had said of the English, the individual under a representative government is free only during a general election. The legislative function, therefore, should be pushed back to the process of participation: of discussion and compromise in local associations.

Barber's conception of strong democracy is precisely what the Idealist political philosophers sought in opposition to and rejection of individualism, with its aim of limited government, as advocated by the Utilitarians, especially John Stuart Mill, and by Herbert Spencer. Green and Bosanquet advocated positive as opposed to negative liberty based on the inherent sociality of human beings, in sympathy and agreement with the Socrates of the *Meno* (insisting that every advantage gained by the citizen is derived from his obedience to the Laws of the *polis*) and with Aristotle's conception of man as a political animal.

Compare the following passages from Barber's *Strong Democracy*,

> ...strong democracy resists the liberal idea that conflict is intractable and at best vulnerable only to adjudication or toleration. Instead, it develops a politics that can transform conflict into cooperation through citizen participation, public deliberation, and civic education. Strong democratic theory begins but does not end with conflict: it acknowledges conflict but ultimately transforms rather than accommodates or minimizes it.... It gives to each individual's convictions and beliefs an equal starting place and associates legitimacy with what happens to convictions and beliefs in the course of public talk and action rather than with their prior epistemological status. The legitimacy of a value is thus a feature of its publicness, of how it is refined, changed, or transformed when confronted with a public and the public norms which that public has already legitimized through its politics. Politics in the participatory mode does not choose between or merely ratify values whose legitimacy is a matter of prior record. It makes preferences and opinions earn legitimacy by forcing them to run the gauntlet of public deliberation and public judgment. They emerge not simply legitimized but transformed by the process to which they have been subjected (Op. cit., pp. 135f).

Compare this with what Bosanquet says of the way in which the actual will of the individual is converted into the general will:

> In order to obtain a full statement of what we will, what we want at any moment must at least be corrected and amended by what we want at all other moments; and this cannot be done without also correcting and amending it so as to harmonize it with what others want, which involves an application of the same process to them... Such a process of harmonizing and readjusting a mass of data to bring them into a rational state is what is meant by criticism....
>
> To obtain something which approximates to a real will, then, involves a process of criticism and interpretation, which may be either natural or intellectual; that is to say, it may proceed by "natural selection," through the method of trial and error, or it may be rapidly advanced at favourable moments by the insight of a great mind. But some forwardness in this criticism and interpretation, bringing with it some deposit, so to speak, of objects of volition in which the private will, so far as it is distinguished at all, finds harmony and expansion, must be coeval with social life, and, in short, with humanity.[3]

Again, compare these passages with what Ernest Barker says of democratic government:

It must be a government depending on mutual interchange of ideas, on mutual criticism of the ideas interchanged and on the common and agreed choice of the idea which emerges triumphant from the ordeal of inter-change and criticism. A government depending on such a process can enlist in itself and its own operation the self of every member. It will be self-government: it will square with, and be based upon, the development of personality and individuality in every self. It will be government by the people not as a mass, or as a majority, but as a society of living selves. In that sense it will be a democracy. But it will be a democracy which does not rest on number or mass or quantity. It will be a democracy which rests on the spiritual quality of the process which it disengages and on the value of the process for every participant. That process is, in a word, discussion – discussion of competing ideas, leading to a compromise in which all the ideas are reconciled and which can be accepted by all because it bears the imprint of all.[4]

For Barker, however, as for Bosanquet, this is government proper, not just Civil Society. It is the totality of the institutional structure which de-termines, through its processes of discussion, the law and policies of the legislative body. Without the operation of this legal and governmental process the activity of Civil Society would have neither security nor sig-nificant effect.

Without the centrally constituted legislative function Civil Society, loses its effectuality. It is dependent for its success on the political insti-tutions of government, and for them by itself it is no adequate substi-tute. Barber's proposals (in his final chapter) do not provide what is needed. The cumbersome and protracted system of referenda which he describes would be far from suitable as a method of legislation. Either it would exclude from informed investigation and debate the details of legislative measures that could not properly be put to referenda, or else (as Barber's proposals imply) politics would become the major business of the whole population, leaving nobody sufficient time for the ordinary occupations of life: productive, economic, domestic, or municipal.

Moreover, Barber seems to presuppose the concurrent continued operation of present legislative institutions in America. These are repre-sentative in the sense that Barber deplores and constitute what "thin democratic" liberals regard as a necessary evil, with which Barber wishes to dispense, replacing central government with participatory interchange of opinions and the consequent generation of commonly agreed values (rather than simply complementing government enactments by such in-terchange). But that is neither theoretically advocable nor practicably feasible; and we need to take care that what Barber is recommending may not appear to be more akin than he would tolerate to the conclusion reached by Carl Schmitt.

Legislation has to be centrally enacted, and what private local associations decide may be and usually is diverse requiring some procedure of unification if it is to be translated into a general political policy. When the population of a country is counted in millions this cannot be accomplished by all the people acting as one constituency,[a] and the only method available is to devolve the legislative power to a body of elected representatives from subdivisions of the territory. That this is not an abrogation of personal responsibility is clearly indicated by Ernest Barker's demonstration of the interdependence of the forms and levels of discussion constituting democratic procedures. There is discussion at the level of voluntary associations, and through them among the members of each political party, then between parties during elections, and again between the elected representatives in the legislature; but the discussion among the representatives cannot be confined to the legislative chamber, it must persist between them and their constituents, with whom and with their accepted (for Barber, participatorily created) values their representative must constantly keep in touch.

But, although the defects of modern liberal democracy can in great measure be traced back to origins in the individualistic doctrines of the seventeenth century, by no means all of them can be attributed to the theoretical predispositions involved in the origins of liberal thinking. "Thin democracy" is not totally averse to exchange of opinions, at any rate on methods of limiting government. What is vitally important is the spirit in which discussion takes place, its rationality, the readiness of the participants to respect differing views, their openness to persuasion and compromise, leading to an outcome which is acceptable to all and represents a common will. Such a spirit seems nowadays to be largely absent from political dispute, being replaced (when not altogether neglected through disinterest) by either unshakeable extremism (religious fundamentalism) or partisan intolerance. Political parties (despite the impassioned public statements of their members) are apt to aim at governmental power at the expense of policies genuinely believed to be

---

[a] Barber admits that what he calls "unitary democracy" in distinction from strong democracy, is undesirable and dangerous, because it submerges the individual subject in a consensus that symbolically represents the total community, and in extreme cases (as in Fascism) it may become indistinguishable from totalitarian despotism (Cf. Op. cit., pp. 148-150).

in the public interest. They are too apt to pander to popular whims and temporary prejudices. Our contemporary problem is how to resuscitate a genuine devotion in politicians to their own sincere opinion of the public good, as that has been honed and adjusted by participation in public debate.

Our next task must be to consider how far the criticisms of democracy that have been so powerfully expressed are valid and how far they are ill founded. If they can be justified, how they may be met and the defects of modern political practices remedied. It is a task which may be deferred to the next chapter, where it more properly belongs.

NOTES

---

[1] In what follows I have relied heavily upon William E. Scheuerman's excellent study, *Carl Schmitt: The End of Law* (Lanham MD, New York and Oxford, Rowman and Littlefield, 1999).

[2] *The Crisis of Parliamentary Democracy*, p.35.

[3] *The Philosophical Theory of the State* (London, Macmillan, 1925), pp. 111f.

[4] *Reflections on Government* (Oxford, Oxford University Press, 1942, 1945, 1948), p. 36.

7. Alternatives or Remedies?

Some of the diatribes of writers like Schmitt, Schumpeter and Hayek have sufficient basis in fact to merit serious confrontation by the advocates of liberal democracy. So we may not pass them over as inadmissible simply because those who voice them offer unacceptable alternatives. We must, therefore, preface any investigation of the sources and possible remedies of the defects to which we have already drawn attention by examining the targets of the attacks by such critics to see whether convincing refutations can be offered to their vituperations.

Of the criticisms of liberal democracy set out in the last chapter, the most serious and the one most needing attention is the attack on the principle of the rule of law. The essence of genuine democracy is the equality of all persons before the law. This tradition has been recognized in England for centuries, where not even royalty is specially privileged, as is witnessed by Shakespeare's representation in *Henry IV* (Part II) of the conviction of Prince Hal by the Lord Chief Justice. Further, it is essential that citizens be assured that the government will refrain from arbitrary action, a confidence that can be relied on only if the administration is required to abide by generally accepted and approved norms set out by the law, primarily constitutional. As was acknowledged by the more important theories of democracy summarized in Chapters I and II, the Constitution has come to be recognized as legally the effective expression of the sovereign *demos* in the modern democratic state. If the critics are right that constitutional law can exercise no genuine normative control over the conduct of the executive, the rule of law becomes inoperative and there can be no interdiction of dictatorship. When Schmitt declares (quoting Montesquieu) that the constituent power is omnipotent he seems to overlook the fact that the true constituent power is the people, either represented by a popularly elected constituent assembly or expressed in a referendum on the draft made by an appointed body, and their authority is thus transferred to the constitution. The question remains whether constitutional law loses its normative character on that account, or whether obedience to the sovereign will of the people is not thereby all the more obligatory.

In any organized society the conduct of its members must be controlled by rules of some sort. These are embodied in the law of the land and such laws, if they are liable to be disobeyed, must be enforced. Accordingly, there must be some governing agency which resorts when necessary to a measure of force to ensure that the law is effective: in general this agency is the government in power. But the power, if the rights of citizens are to be protected, must be restrained from capricious and arbitrary action. While the law is enacted by the legislature, the police and the law courts with their related agencies enforce it. These departments of the governing executive, if they are not to be oppressive, must be trusted to act within clearly recognized limits, i.e. under the rule of law.

The rule of law is not understood in quite the same way in all democratic countries, yet it always has the same general import: namely, that the officers of the administration, be they cabinet ministers, police, or members of other administrative agencies, are constrained to act within limits prescribed by recognized legal rules. These rules must of necessity be normative, or they would not be rules governing conduct at all, nor in any proper sense law. If law does not exercise any normative force on its subjects, it ceases to be positive law and becomes at best a theory or an academic concept. The kernel of the argument of critics like Schmitt is that law in general, because of its unavoidably indeterminate character, cannot be normative and can never exercise any restraint over the executive power. In effect they deny that there is any law at all as generally and properly understood. If then the rule of law is to be saved from such abrogation, our first task must be to show that the law is not crippled by the fact of its indeterminacy.

If the term "law" is to have any significant meaning at all it must be that it is a norm. So far Kelsen's assertion is undoubtedly right. That is what the term "law" means: a rule, or body of rules, governing the conduct of members of a community (even if it has other applications in different spheres from politics – e.g., empirical science). It is therefore normative, or it is not law. The law is nothing other than a system of norms prescribing some and prohibiting other types of conduct and procedures. Now a type, or category, is what logicians call a universal, and a universal has both connotation (its definitive character) and denotation (the particulars that conform to the connotation). The connotation is general but not indeterminate. It does not indicate in detail the differentia that distinguish the particulars one from another, but it does determine their specific general character. The number 2 is a universal connoting all couples, but its generality does not make it indeterminate. There is no indeterminacy in the meaning of the number two, although it does not determine whether a couple is of human twins, copies of a document, or contestants in a duel. It is precisely no other number, it is definitely and determinately one less than three and double the number one.

A law pronounces similarly upon the universal character of what it prescribes or prohibits, which does not make it indeterminate except with respect to the differentia of its cases. Accordingly, it is perfectly proper to speak of "subsumption" (that the critics decry) of a particular case under the appropriate law, as we subsume particular couples under the universal, two. What distinguishes one case from others is dependent upon their particular circumstances, and it is the circumstances that make some cases "hard" and others "easy". Schmitt and his followers contend that all cases are of necessity hard cases because of the indeterminacy of the law, failing to understand that generality (universality) does not involve indeterminacy – rather the opposite. Once this is understood the argument that law is indeterminate because of its necessary generality falls to the ground, and the law cannot be disqualified from its normativity on account of alleged indeterminacy. In that case, the diatribe against the rule of law loses its menace and the principle can be reinstated. Normativity is not sacrificed simply because the law is enacted by parliamentary vote (held by Schmitt to be arbitrary "willing" contradictory of normativity). Such enactment, on the contrary, because Parliament is the designated political body with authority to legislate, is what gives the law its normative imperative as well as its positivity. Parliament's authority is, moreover, conditional upon its devotion to the common welfare of the nation – a norm that legitimizes that of the law itself.

The allegation made by Schmitt is unfounded that the decision of a judge is always inevitably discretionary because there is no possible norm to guide him in his interpretation of the law when deciding a particular case. His knowledge of the law and of precedents should be sufficient and he would have no need to speculate about how other judges would decide, except insofar as he deferred to their superior learning. Not infrequently judges disagree as to the interpretation of the relevant law. That is why, sometimes, in specially complicated and difficult cases, it is desirable to have three or five judges presiding over the proceedings of the court, so that the decision can be made by majority vote.

Next, the description given by Schmitt of the total state needs to be examined. True it is that the welfare state involves intervention by government in various practices adopted by the different associations that make up society. These include the nationalization of health care,[a] the provision of unemployment benefit, social welfare, government support of the needy, and the provision by the state of old age pensions, health and safety regulations, as well as, where necessary, other forms of intervention regulating transport and commercial practices. Such intervention is primarily directed towards the prevention of hardship, the counteraction of injustices and of unacceptable inequalities in the treatment of persons – they are what Bosanquet called hindrances of hindrances to freedom. As such, government intervention is not a form of dictatorship nor a possible invitation to it, but is the condition of the positive liberty that is, and ought to be, the typical aim of democratic rule.

The accusation that the codes of civil and human rights are purely relative to the historical period and to differing cultures has some validity, but it does not make them altogether futile. In the first place they establish a principle. Their recognition by the government of a state serves as a protection to its citizens from despotism of the worst kind, even if their variations from one culture to another may give rise to difficulties in international relations. That, however, has other and more serious causes than mere relativity, to which we shall return anon.

The disparagement of the notion of the common good as mythological and as a cover for the competition of political parties for power is admissible so far as it is a criticism of the conduct of politicians in our time; but there can be no doubt that the idea itself is a feasible concept with objective significance. Nobody can seriously question the facts that an efficient and well organized transport system is beneficial to the public, or that a well-run and hygienic health service is in the interests of the entire population of any society, as likewise are measures to reduce

---

[a] This does not legitimize government interference with professional decisions and the organization of professional bodies and activities.

or eliminate poverty. The questions why contemporary politicians fail to address such needs of society, and to withstand pressures from business interests or the demands of popular prejudice, and why they disguise their mutual opposition by talking (when they do) of seeking the public welfare, are a different matter that we may investigate in due course – one that does not impugn the validity of the philosophical conception of a common good, and if politicians do not in fact pursue that end, it is a fault attributable to them, not to the idea itself.

Having disposed of these criticisms of liberal democracy, we can now consider others less specious, as well as the deficiencies to which our own observations have drawn attention, and seek an answer to the question how they may be overcome. Some of them overlap with those derided by Schmitt and others who have adopted a similar stance, but the alternative Schmitt approves is so repugnant that we can but reject it on sight. If modern professedly democratic states have failed, or are failing, to realize the conception of popular self-government that the philosophers of the past had developed, the question arises whether there is any alternative form of polity that could be substituted for what presently passes for democracy or, if not, what remedies, if any, might be available.

It is clear that no form of despotism is desirable, not even an enlightened absolute sovereignty, such as Plato's philosopher kingship. Philosophers today are no more reliably competent to govern than are popularly elected politicians. They are by no means all in agreement; there are numerous different schools of philosophy (as there always have been); academic discussion among them, even when sincere and genuinely considerate of differences of opinion, is commonly inconclusive; one recent school even rejected political philosophy altogether, as mere ideology and not truly philosophy at all. Nor has administrative ability commonly accompanied reflective inspiration.

Clearly Plato was right to insist that the rulers should be those who are properly educated and best qualified to judge, but how are they to be selected? One might propose a form of appointment similar to that adopted by universities, based on academic achievement, but administrative ability and experience are just as important. Or a method of election, similar to that of the Pope, traditional in the Roman Catholic Church, by an Electoral College the members of which had been appointed by former rulers. The crucial issue is to identify those who should make the selection, if not the people who are to be subject to the governing person or body, who and how selected? If they are to be appointees of the retiring or deceased philosopher kings, can these be trusted to make the best choice? Plato himself failed dismally in his attempt to establish a philosopher as king in Syracuse; and Plato is no longer with us. If he were, would we still regard his as the right ordainment? To leave supreme power solely in the hands of one person is always risky, because, however wise and well educated, he or she is unlikely to be able to comprehend unfailingly what is good for and will satisfy the people of an entire nation. That can be reliably ascertained only by widespread consultation and discussion among citizens belonging to different social classes (and possibly also ethnicities).

All forms of oligarchy are seriously liable to concentrate power in the hands of special and vested interests, which are seldom if ever those of the majority of the subject people. So we seem committed to Winston Churchill's conclusion, that democracy, however distorted, is better than any other form of government. If so, our attention must be directed to remedying defects rather than substitution for the overall structure of government. What might the remedies be?

If modern democracy is to be restored to what was envisaged by early twentieth century thinkers certain fundamental principles must be respected, the first and most important of which is the maintenance of the rule of law, not only within the national state, but equally in the relations between national states. The latter cannot be enforced at present because the claim to sovereignty by the national state exempts it from subjection to any higher legislation – and so-called International Law can only be enforced against sovereign regimes (if at all) by waging war, which is itself a breach of the rule of law (besides, nowadays, with the possible use of nuclear weapons, being a self-defeating expedient). Within state governments the tendency to politicize the judiciary seems to be the consequence of an impermissible desire on the part of politicians for arbitrary powers that the judges will not question, indicating a growing tendency, that has been encouraged by the fear of terrorism, to evade the rule of law.

Implicit in the above principle are certain subordinate, but no less significant principles of democracy: the first is the equality of all persons before the law, permitting no special privileges or favors; the second is *habeas corpus*, the rule that no person be imprisoned without charge, prosecution, and conviction of an offence; and third is the presumption that accused persons are innocent until they have been proved guilty by a court after due process of law. The next most important principle is that civil and human rights are indefeasible, and must be respected and protected. The establishment is required of a constitutional system of surveillance on behalf of the citizens to detect and prevent corruption, and the abuse of power, and to outlaw arbitrary authoritarian dictatorship. Finally, the law of the Constitution must be supreme – but the articles of the Constitution should be periodically reviewed, in the light of public discussion, and, if desirable, amended by the duly elected legislative body (or bodies).

Having listed these requirements we must further consider, not simply how contemporary democracy has forsaken its traditional ideals, but also the global conditions in which it is called upon to function. Since the philosophical theories reviewed in former chapters became current the world situation has altered so drastically as to make it necessary to reconsider the needs and objectives of social order in the light of new circumstances that are unprecedented. Not only has the world and its peoples endured the ravages of the most destructive and costly wars in their history, but at the end of the Second World War new weapons were developed of more devastating destructive power than had ever before been conceived: atomic bombs, and, their enhancement, hydrogen bombs. Only once have nuclear weapons been used in combat: the atom bombs dropped on Hiroshima and Nagasaki which brought World War II to an end. But subsequently the major victorious combatants armed themselves with nuclear arsenals sufficient, if used, to destroy all earthly civilizations. As noted above, scientists have predicted that a major nuclear exchange would not simply wreck cities and the infrastructures of the warring countries, but would cause climatic disturbances producing a "nuclear winter" – a new ice age – making civilized life virtually impossible anywhere on the planet. Meanwhile, quite apart from this dire prospect, yet largely resulting from human activities, industrial and other, the widespread use of fossil fuels is polluting the Earth's atmosphere with greenhouse gases (primarily carbon dioxide) which cause global warming. This is already disrupting the planetary environment to an extent that threatens to destroy the unique atmospheric and climatic conditions peculiar to the Earth that are delicately and astonishingly adapted to the needs of life and are essential to its continuance. It is also modifying the movement of ocean currents which determine climate, and acidifying sea-water making it lethal to plankton, the basic level of the food chain. It is melting the polar ice-caps, raising the levels of the oceans so as to threaten with inundation half the population of the earth which lives on low lying islands and coasts. The human race is now faced with problems menacing its survival which it has never be-

fore experienced, so that the social order rationally developed throughout the ages, what Aristotle recognized as having come into existence to
ensure the bare means of life and persisting in existence for the sake of
the good life, is now teetering on the brink of final catastrophe.

To meet this perilous situation the means of preserving the conditions of "the good life" or of any life whatsoever need to be reconsid-
ered, and the political practices which have become customary in the
developed democracies need to be reassessed, both as to their appropriateness to the traditionally recognized aims of civil organization and as
to their competence to meet the currently overshadowing world crises.

Meanwhile, the effect in the international sphere of the prevalent
relations between sovereign states, in which war has been endemic ever
since the sixteenth century, has led to increasing and more destructive
conflicts. That enmity and war between sovereign states is inevitable has
been recognized by political theorists from Hobbes to Hegel and, as we
have seen, by several more contemporary writers. As far as sovereign
nations are concerned, Schmitt's assessment of the concept of the political is not in error. Morgenthau also realized that in the international
arena "neither science nor ethics nor politics can resolve the conflict between politics and ethics into harmony." This is so because sovereign
independence necessarily implies an overriding interest in security and
the deterrence of possible aggression by foreign powers. Consequently,
states have given paramount attention to defense: to strengthening their
arsenals, the accumulation and augmentation in destructive power
of their weapons, striving to increase that of their own in order at least
to match those of their potential enemies and if possible to surpass
them. Weaker powers seek safety in alliances under the protection of the
stronger. The result has been a general attempt to maintain a balance of
power between opposing blocs – a balance which constantly breaks
down as technology advances and governments strive to ensure their
ability to deter aggression and to resist invasion. There ensues an ever
accelerating arms race impossible to check, with intermittent international tensions, which lead to progressively increasing crises and to minor wars, tending towards more and more widespread conflict.

This has been the pattern of history in the west ever since the
14ᵗʰ century, through the succession of wars in the 18ᵗʰ century that cul-
minated in the Napoleonic conquests. It continued throughout the 19ᵗʰ
century with a sequence of minor conflicts which escalated in 1914 to
the outbreak of the Great War, and again, twenty-five years later, to the
Second World War. There succeeded a stand-off between the two re-

maining major powers: the USA and the USSR, in a Cold War that almost erupted in a devastating nuclear holocaust when the Soviets proceeded to erect missile bases in Cuba, and finally subsided only when the Soviet Union collapsed towards the end of the twentieth century. We are now left with a single super-power exercising world hegemony, threatening to impose its own policies on all other states, with scant regard for the wishes of other peoples as expressed in the councils of the United Nations. The United States prides itself on its deference to democracy, but its present superiority in power over all other nations induces it to disregard many of the principles listed above, whenever its administration considers that its national interests are threatened. The hegemony of a single nation, however, may be only temporary, depending on the extent that the most populous nations in the world, China and India, can increase their wealth and augment their arsenals. If they become powerful enough to challenge the United States, the world situation will return to its previous prevailing condition of competition among these states to maintain the balance of power, a balance that has never been stable, with the consequent persistent tendency to generate tensions and open conflict – a state of affairs that, since the development of modern weapons of mass destruction, has become intolerable. This parlous situation is the direct consequence of the claim to sovereignty of the nations of the world, a claim that admits no law superior to its own, and which gives unquestioning priority to national interests, especially those regarded as "vital", namely, first and foremost, security from foreign aggression, and secondly economic prosperity. Sovereignty, Professor George Keeton rightly maintained, is the evil genius of international affairs.

Neither International Law nor the United Nations can ameliorate this state of affairs. International Law lays down as its first principle that its sole subjects are sovereign states, and then defines sovereign states as those which acknowledge no legislation superior to their own, thus annulling its own authority. The common practice of states bears out this definition, for they ignore, violate and defy the rules of International Law whenever they conflict with their perceived national interests, or they interpret them to suit their own purposes. Sovereign states refuse to recognize the jurisdiction of the International Court of Justice and the International Criminal Court whenever they affect their citizens or unfavorably bear upon their actions (the United States has done so on several occasions, as have other nations). The international principle that treaties should be observed has throughout history frequently been ignored and violated.

The United Nations, incidentally, is anything but democratic. It is simply a forum for diplomatic negotiation. Being constrained by Article 2 of its Charter to respect and uphold the sovereign independence of its members, it has proved as impotent to prevent wars as its predecessor, the League of Nations – in fact it has no means of doing so other than those prescribed in Chapter VII of its Charter, namely, taking all measures "by land, sea and air" – in short, by making war! There are some who advocate reform of the international body to make it "more democratic" by the addition of a second Assembly, to advise the General Assembly, the members of which would either be popularly elected or selected from popularly elected parliamentarians. In the unlikely event that none of the permanent members of the Security Council veto such reform, it could not have the desired result, because the second Assembly would be only advisory to the first, which is itself only advisory. Neither could have any legislative power as long as the nations remain sovereign, independent and subject to no superior legislation. The Assembly (or Assemblies) could thus never be anything more than consultative and advisory to the Security Council, and the resolutions of the Security Council may be (and often have been) defied by any of the sovereign member states which find them contrary to their perceived national interests. There is no available method of compulsion other than war, for which Chapter VII of the United Nations Charter itself provides. Economic sanctions not only have effects, if any, which are very slow and which cause suffering among the populace rather than persuasion of the delinquent government, but they need to be backed by military measures to prevent violation and rarely have any effect at all without military backing.

Along with other flash-points in the contemporary world, the state of Israel is one of the worst. Ever since the Zionist campaign of terrorism against the British at the end of World War II and the subsequent internationally recognized independence of Israel in 1947, Israeli governments (at times inspired by Biblical promises) have continuously pursued a chauvinistic and self-centered policy of eviction and oppression towards the Palestinians, paying little respect to their legitimate rights in their own homeland. (Incidentally, acknowledging these facts has nothing to do with anti-Semitism. If one deplores them one is criticizing policies, not race or religion). Such policies have provoked a holy war (*Jihad*) against Israel among Arab and other Muslim sympathizers with the Palestinians, the first military outbreaks of which failed, in large measure because of American and other western support given to the

Israelis, not simply moral and political but material with the supply of arms. Thus weakened, the Palestinians and their allies have resorted to terrorist tactics, suicide bombings encouraged by religious belief in the rewards of martyrdom in an afterlife. By their consistent support of the state of Israel, the United States and, to a lesser degree, the European Union, have provoked the antagonism of several Arab states and other Muslim countries, extending the *Jihad* into a system of clandestine and widespread indiscriminate terrorism that threatens all parts of the world. This global threat, however, is only one of those that menace the human race today, none of which can be addressed or remedied within the existing structure of international relations. It is one that is intensified by the various forms of fundamentalism that have been described in Chapter IV, which, along with the mutual opposition of sovereign nations, emphasizes the relativity of different conceptions, such as they may be, of human rights.

Adding to these perils, overshadowing all of them, the rapidly increasing environmental deterioration with its menaces to the very terrestrial conditions that support life, human and all other, and the failure of every attempt so far made to bring about concerted international measures to check and remedy ecological destruction, make it clear that we have urgent need to discern the causes of our present predicament. One of the most impressive, and indeed the most alarming, among recent books dealing with environmental disruption is James G. Speth's *Red Sky at Morning*.[a] His account and analysis of the ominous threats of global warming and climate change, with the accompanying loss of species and terrestrial productivity, are both authoritative and no less than terrifying. He stresses the failure of international endeavors to reach agreement on the necessary remedial measures, which are quite easily available, and are urgently needed, and he recognizes (at least by implication) that the main cause of this failure is the constant priority given by sovereign governments to national and economic interests over environmental needs. I shall select just a few quotations.

---

[a] James Gustav Speth, dean and professor at the School of Forestry and Environment in Yale University, is founder and was President of the World Resources Institute, co-founder of the National Resources Defense Council, served as adviser on environmental issues for Presidents Carter and Clinton, and was chief executive officer of the United Nations Development Program.

Between 1950 and 1985 the U.S. chemical industry expanded its output ten-fold. By 1985 the number of hazardous waste sites in the United States requiring clean-up was estimated to be between two thousand and ten thousand. The use of pesticides skyrocketed during this period. Today about six hundred pesticides are registered for use around the world, and five to six billion pounds of pesticides are released into the global environment each year.

Turning from pollution to the world's natural resource base we find severe losses. From a third to a half of the world's forests are now gone, as are about half the mangroves and other wetlands. Agricultural productivity of a fourth of all usable land has been significantly degraded due to overuse and mismanagement. In 1960, 5 percent of marine fisheries were either fished to capacity or over-fished; today 75 percent of marine fisheries are in this condition. A crisis in the loss of bio-diversity is fast upon us. A fourth of bird species are extinct, and another 12 percent are listed as threatened. Also threatened are 24 percent of mammals, 25 percent of reptiles, and 30 percent of fish species. The rate of species extinction today is estimated to be a hundred to a thousand times the normal rate at which species disappear (pp. 14f).

In international negotiations, sovereign nations are represented at the table, and sovereignty means that no country is required to accept the will of the majority or be obligated without its consent. Whereas most congressional decisions require agreement by a majority…international agreements, to the degree that they are to be effective, must secure the agreement of essentially every country that is important to the outcome (100 percent, p. 103).

The weakness of current international environmental treaties should thus come as no surprise. They were forged in cumbersome negotiating processes that give maximum leverage to any country with an interest in protecting the status quo. The United States successfully weakened the Kyoto Protocol, Brazil worked to keep the forest convention at bay, and Japan and other major fishing countries watered down the international marine fisheries agreement (pp. 104f).

[T]he inherently weak political base for international action is typically overrun by economic opposition and protection of sovereignty (p. 116).

The European Union …has boldly plunged into the thicket and has concluded that it would be 'dangerous' to allow global average temperatures to increase by more than 2⁰ C over the pre-industrial level…To achieve this goal, the European Union estimates that a global reduction in greenhouse gas emissions of 50 to 60 percent by 2050 will be needed… [T]he climate goals being discussed in Europe, as stringent as they are, may not be stringent enough. Moreover, a global average temperature increase of 2⁰ C could turn out to be quite 'dangerous' and not safe at all... a warming of 2^0 C globally could translate into twice or more than that at the poles, with serious consequences there and elsewhere. Coral Systems would be severely affected; terrestrial and coastal ecosystems would suffer; the ranges of many diseases would change; more extreme weather events would occur; and so on. A world with another 1.4^0 C global average warming is not a world for which one would wish, and yet right now we are on track to produce a world in far worse shape, and we are moving down that track very rapidly (pp. 210ff.)

The prevalent consumerism of the western world that has developed since the growth of global capitalism has contributed in no small degree to this environmental deterioration. On the assumption that the population of the world will continue to increase at the current rate, it has been estimated that to provide the people of the developing world with the average standard of living of the developed nations (to which the immense populations of China and India are now rapidly approaching) would require three times the resources of the planet Earth. Even today these resources are being used up so rapidly that they are expected to give out within the next century. Consequently, only a drastic reform of the way of living of contemporary civilized nations will save humanity from final disaster.

Earlier theories of political order, as we have seen, based the internal sovereignty of the state upon two principles, the majesty and supremacy of the law, and the service of the common good by the government (the first being conditional upon the second). Externally, these two principles have, up to the present, necessitated independence, freedom from domination by a foreign power and consequent defense against aggression. It follows that all sovereign states will be, at least potentially, when they are not actually, enemies. As Hobbes declared, they constantly have "their weapons pointing and their eyes fixed on one another... and continually Spies upon their neighbors; which is a posture of War"[1] – a posture still prevalent at the present day. Even allies may at times disagree, and disagreements cause tensions which in extreme cases can blow up into threats, so that allies may in such circumstances change sides. Warfare is consequently an ever-present prospect among sovereign states – a prospect that in the modern age of nuclear weapons is altogether insufferable.

The central cause of the daunting contemporary situation is at base the continued existence and practical exercise of sovereign rights by the nations, which has itself become a menace to genuine democracy, because not all states are even professedly democratic, and many, while they claim immunity from outside interference, fail to respect civil and human rights; and in those that are formally democracies, democratic principles are threatened by the measures taken to increase security against terrorism: for example, the introduction of indeterminate detention of terrorist suspects without charge, the abolition of *habeas corpus* and of jury trials in suspected terrorist cases. The American President has declared "war on global terrorism" and both the United States and Britain have already, in their attack on Iraq, shown a preference for pre-emptive aggression without authorization by the United Nations' Security Council.

It is not to be overlooked that International Law is incurably ineffective. Inspired though it was in the seventeenth century by the mediaeval doctrine of Natural Law that had been identified with the law of reason and the Law of God, it has always remained more of an aspiration than positive enforceable law. Unenforceable it must be by its very nature, as it admits no subjects other than sovereign states, which it defines as recognizing no superior legislation. In actual practice states – even those that are generally considered democratic and "law-abiding" – interpret International Law to suit themselves and submit to no court that does otherwise. Even the jurisdiction of the International Court of Justice is rejected by sovereign states whenever they think fit; cases are brought before it only with the consent of the disputants and its decision may be and often is, even then, repudiated by parties that find it obnoxious, being at variance with what they consider their "vital interests." The recent establishment of an International Criminal Court has not been ratified by as many nations as requisite and has been formally rejected by the United States, while other nations are always liable to denounce its jurisdiction if they see in it a threat to the conduct of their own citizens which they have not themselves condemned. It is true of International Law that, although its demands are normative, in practice it exercises little or no normative function, not because it is indeterminate (although in some respects it is that also), but because it contradicts itself by defining its sole subjects as sovereign and exempt from any superior legislative authority.

Sovereign governments ignore or violate the provisions of International Law with impunity, as has the USA most recently in the treatment of prisoners taken in the Afghan war and imprisoned in Guantanamo Bay. In fact, no law (other than their own) can be enforced on sovereign states except by military conquest, or by economic sanctions, (which are ineffective and liable to be broken unless backed by the threat of military action, and then succeed, when they do, only after long delays). War, however, is itself a violation of the Rule of Law, being a resort to the rule of naked force. Yet war, as we have observed, is endemic among sovereign states. Since the development of nuclear weapons, moreover, war has become an intolerably perilous instrument of policy, because it cannot be won (despite the contentions of Hermann Kahn and the "optimistic" plans for pre-emptive attack contemplated in the 1960s by the Pentagon), as both assailant and assailed equally would be destroyed if only by the immediate devastation of the explosions and their long-term radio-active fall-out (not to mention the resulting climate change and possible "nuclear winter"). Yet the unavoidable resort to military threats and belligerent action by the powers whenever crises occur inevitably involves the possibility of escalation threatening, when the situation of either of the warring parties seems desperate, to explode in a nuclear holocaust enveloping the entire world in irremediable destruction.

This menace has not been removed since the end of the Cold War, because not only have the nuclear powers retained the bulk of their nuclear arsenals but lesser regimes have (either clandestinely or openly) acquired nuclear capability (e.g., India, Pakistan, and Israel) while others (like North Korea and possibly Iran) are threatening to develop it, and there is no way to stop this proliferation except the resort to war itself which involves the ultimate threat. Diplomacy cannot finally ensure success, whatever result it may achieve, because sovereign states observe their international commitments only so far as those commitments conform to what they regard as their vital interests; and, furthermore, any coup or change of government may incur a policy change involving the renunciation, or simple violation, of what has formerly been internationally agreed. At the same time, the ever-present danger exists that nuclear material will fall into the hands of terrorists giving them access to so-called "dirty bombs" or worse.

Meanwhile, human activity (the emission of greenhouse gases by industries, aircraft and motor vehicles, and the general use of fossil fuels, the unchecked destruction of tropical forests, the pollution of the oceans, and fishing techniques that destroy the breeding beds of plankton) is depleting the resources of the earth, accelerating global warming, and rapidly advancing climate change. The consequent shrinking of the polar ice-caps is predicted to raise sea-levels sufficiently to submerge low-lying islands and coastal areas many of which are densely populated. Most of the greatest cities are in this situation, for example, New York,

Boston, London, Liverpool, Tokyo, and all major seaports. Further, climate change, besides depriving countless species of the habitats in which they can survive, causes increased desertification and widespread crop failures threatening human populations with famine, while the decline of the water-table in many areas, due to lack of rainfall and the demands of increased industrial activity, leads to a shortage of fresh water, the consequent spread of disease, and threatening tensions between neighboring states which depend on the same water sources.

The chief scientific adviser to the British Government, Sir David King, has warned that climate change is a more serious threat to the security of the world than terrorism, because it will affect millions of people the world over with drought, famine, flooding and extreme meteorological upheavals, many of which are already being experienced.

A leaked report from the Pentagon to President Bush has predicted that the calamitous effects of global warming will drive mass migrations that will be resisted by neighboring countries igniting new wars and prompting nations that have access to weapons of mass destruction to use them. Hence the problems of maintaining world peace and of conserving the global ecological system are interlinked and are both rendered insoluble as long as the nations remain and claim to be sovereign and independent.

Successive "summit" conferences, called to decide on ways to conserve the environment have failed, after much difficult and dissentient negotiation, to produce anything better than non-binding agreements (which many states have rejected, including the most powerful),[a] to adopt measures that are hopelessly inadequate, and which to date are not widely being implemented even by those who have acceded to them. Yet no measures can be of any avail unless adopted globally, for what any one government undertakes will be futile if others neglect to follow suit or act in contradictory ways. The reason for the failure of concerted international action and of seeming national insouciance is, once again, that sovereign states inevitably give precedence over ecological requirements to what they see as their national interests. Economic development is given priority by the developed industrialized countries, while the less developed resent being required to make sacrifices for the envi-

---

[a] President George W. Bush withdrew the United States from the Kyoto Protocol on climate change, claiming that it was not in the economic interests of the country. His close links with the petro-chemical industry of Texas is as likely to have been his motive. But then the interests of that industry and the economic requirements of the nation are hardly distinguishable.

ronmental misconduct of the richer nations and to forego industrialization from which the developed states have benefited disproportionately.

The same dilatoriness and reluctance to act as world conditions
demand has been displayed by the G8 nations with regard to the ration-
alization of world economics, so as to eliminate the great contrast between the rich developed countries and those desperately poor and still
under-developed, mostly in Africa. Promises of debt relief have been
postponed; targets for aid agreed upon by the more important members
of the European Union to be reached by 2010 (itself much too late) are
as yet markedly lower than the 15 year overdue promise to allocate 0.7%
of national income; and there is little or no inclination to reform the
world economic system, by reducing or eliminating agricultural subsidies
in the wealthier countries which militate against exports from the
poorer, such as Mozambique, the West African, Caribbean and South
American states, and threaten with collapse their efforts at recovery. The
reason for this delay and insensitivity to the evils of poverty in the third
world is nothing other than concern for the special interests of the
farmers and national economies of the richer nations – another consequence of the self-interest of sovereign independent states.

My purposes in emphasizing and elaborating upon the really terrifying problems with which humanity is now faced are, first, that so few
people recognize them or their true causes, and that among those who
do many tend to discount them in the belief that they will not be affected by them; secondly, that the ever-present obstruction to any solution of international problems, namely, the persistence of national sovereignty and its inevitable consequences, is scarcely ever admitted. This
leads directly to the conclusion that national sovereign states at the present time can no longer ensure to their own peoples the security that
they originally promised and that was the essential justification of their
raison d'etre.

In short, the sovereign nation state, whatever its form of government and, however democratic it professes to be, can no longer achieve
the objective of social organization: namely, the welfare and security of
its people. Its constant vigilance against possible attack from without,
and the consequent arms-race that ensues between it and its potential
enemies makes eventual war virtually inevitable, from which it cannot
keep its people safe, because it cannot protect them from destruction,
there being no effective defense against the weapons that may be used
against it, nor can it protect them against the rapidly advancing climate
changes that threaten to destroy the conditions of healthy living, because

nothing that it does or refrains from doing within the limits of its own jurisdiction will be sufficient unless all other states do likewise. As the sole condition on which sovereign power can be legitimized is that it can maintain the conditions of the good life, strictly speaking the nation-state is no longer the legitimate bearer of sovereign authority. As long as national states remain sovereign, such democracy as exists (whether only professedly or more genuinely) is endangered internally by the extreme measures adopted to meet exceptional global menaces (such as terrorism and war), and externally by those dangers themselves, as well as others arising from global warming.

Consequently, contemporary government (democratic or other) is government motivated by fear: fear of foreign aggression, fear of inter-national terrorism, fear of economic decline, fear of starvation when crops fail because of climate change, fear of unjust discrimination (racial, religious, or political: e.g., in Palestine), fear of religious apostasy (e.g., in Iran), and fear of genocide (e.g. by the Chechens). These fears prompt activities that erode away the principles and characteristic features of genuine democracy in countries where that has been a long tradition, while in undemocratic countries where religious tradition has been dominant such principles have not been respected. If these fears could be removed (or at least reduced), possibly true democracy might be regenerated in those nations in which it is showing signs of decay, and made more attractive to such nations as are without it. For this rea-son, besides others that are no less weighty, the perilous world situation that has emerged in the twenty-first century may not be overlooked in any consideration of the possible correction of the defects that have de-veloped in contemporary democratic practice. Only if the dangers cur-rently overshadowing the human race can be removed and the associated world problems effectively tackled will there be any pros-pect of regenerating the democratic idea.

NOTES

---

[1] Hobbes, T., *Leviathan*, (Oxford, Clarendon Press, 1909-1943), Ch. 13, p.98.

8. The Global Solution

The main problems with which the nations must contend if genuine democracy is to be restored may be listed as follows:

1 Current theories of market forces and their alleged beneficial economic and social effects – the widespread adoption of the views of Hayek, what may be called in general "Thatcherism" The consequence of this practice has resulted in the global dominance by transnational corporations, not only of national economies, but also of political policies (often clandestine).
2 Indiscriminate, world-wide terrorism.
3 Consequent disregard for basic legal principles such as *habeas corpus* and the provisions of the Hague Convention to which states have hitherto been committed.
4 Failure to maintain the rule of law, both within national governments, and in international affairs.
5 The effects of global warming and climate change.
6 Failure of universal respect for human and civil rights.
7 The constantly swelling numbers of refugees and asylum seekers, the consequence of (ii) and (v) above, in particular of desertification and famine produced by climate change.
8 The international drugs traffic.
9 The inevitable arms race, due to the concern of independent national sovereign states about security, which produces tensions and international crises, threatening war tending to escalate into world-war with weapons of mass destruction.

These are almost all global problems, few of which can be solved by measures taken (when, if ever, they are) by individual nation-states, if only because their jurisdiction is limited to their own territories, and what other nations do, or neglect to do, affects them no less than what they themselves enact. It follows that solutions will require concentration of political power in some other form than the national sovereign state.

The theory of democratic self-government developed by nineteenth and twentieth century philosophers has not been refuted. Its appeal and its analysis of actual democratic practice are more convincing than the academic criticisms that have been leveled against it. But in twenty-first century world conditions it is not sustainable because the national sovereign state can no longer fulfill the function that was its *raison d'etre*: namely, ensuring the security of its citizens, protecting their human and civil rights, and maintaining of the rule of law. The national state is, therefore, no longer the legitimate claimant of sovereignty. Where now can that claim be justified?

At the present time, the two fundamental principles justifying national sovereignty – the supporting pillars of sovereign power and authority – the rule of law and the pursuit of the common good of its subjects, have been undermined, so that national sovereignty, as such, has become obsolete. Democracy, the sovereignty of the people, can no longer be claimed by separate national groups, because, as such, they can no longer maintain these two fundamental conditions. Ever since their origin in Europe in the fourteenth and fifteenth centuries, national sovereigns have assumed a mutual posture of potential or actual hostility; but before the twentieth century, warfare, cruel and destructive though it has ever been, has not been totally annihilating, as in the twenty-first century it has potentially become, so that national governments no longer have the means to protect their populations from the wholesale effects of weapons of mass destruction. Likewise, since the industrial revolution, human activities have progressively been polluting the earth's atmosphere so that climate change throughout the world as a whole is threatening the survival of living beings; and this cannot be remedied by national governments with jurisdiction limited to their own borders.

It is thus clear that under the currently existing world conditions the traditional conception of democracy, whether in the form envisaged by the individualistic thinkers of the seventeenth to nineteenth centuries or that entertained by later idealistic philosophers, cannot be realized. What they conceived as the necessary condition of the exercise of sovereign

power in the state – its service of the common good – has become un-
sustainable within the national state. National sovereignty, the unavoidable source of conflict, has become the evil genius of international relations, in which successive tensions threaten wars with weapons of universal destruction and have rendered the modern state incompetent to
protect its subjects from imminent death, and similarly the widespread
use of fossil fuels by the developed countries is destroying the terrestrial
environment, so that separate national regimes cannot protect their peoples from the ravages of climate change (of which the pursuit of national
interests in economic growth is itself largely the cause).

In the world today the only form of democracy that could aspire to
the ideals of the traditional philosophical conception would have to be
global, one that could legislate to implement global measures to deal
with global problems (as sovereign nation-states cannot) and could
maintain the Rule of Law world-wide (which the exercise of sovereign
rights by independent nations prevents). Accordingly, the only effective democracy would have to take the form of World Government, and
that can be truly democratic only if it is federal, because federalism as-
sures the right of member states to autonomy with respect to their own
internal affairs, while it consigns to the federal administration control
over issues, the interest in which is common to all its peoples, and which
the several member states cannot regulate within their own jurisdiction.

Federal government has been a subject of discussion and dispute
ever since Hamilton and Madison debated the topic in the latter decades
of the eighteenth century. It took statutory form in the Constitution of
the United States of America, which has survived as a viable political
structure to the present day. The same is true of other federations like
those of Switzerland, Canada, Australia, and more recently India. Its
possible success, therefore, cannot be questioned. The United States is
the most spectacular example (and today the most powerful), but other
federal states offer diverse examples of eminently stable and prosperous
forms.

The motivations that impel states to federate are usually (i) a common external threat (in the American instance, it was the presence in
Canada of the British power, from which the other colonies had just
won their independence). Further strong influential considerations are
(ii) a common language and social tradition; (iii) previous membership of
an empire, a confederation or loose commonwealth of nations; (iv) some
degree of economic interdependence; (v) the disadvantages of rivalry in
commerce, the inconvenience of differing and unstable currencies along

with the cost and uncertainty of national defense; and (vi) the availability of efficient means of communication and transport, all of which amount to a common interest in the pursuit of compatible domestic and commercial policies.

The nations of the world today face common threats greater and more dramatic than ever before, so they ought acutely to feel the first of the above urges towards union. At least a verbal recognition of democracy as a common tradition is widely acknowledged. Apart from Esperanto, English is fast becoming the *linqua franca* of the entire world. The nations have been members of a form of confederation for almost a century (first the League of Nations and, since 1945, the United Nations). The economic interdependence of all the nations of the world today is marked and undeniable: what happens on the stock exchange in New York affects what happens in Tokyo, and the wage-rate in the Far East affects employment in Europe; America and Europe depend on oil supplies from the Middle East, Nigeria, Russia and elsewhere; the manufactured products of the west, of Japan and China, and increasingly of India, are exported world-wide and the agricultural products of South America, the West Indies and Africa are consumed in Europe (these are but selected examples). A major cause of the parlous situation in which states are now embroiled (economic rivalry, unstable currencies, vast costliness of national defense) is the next of the conditions listed above and the means of virtually instant communication world-wide is now available by radio, satellite-transmitted telephony and the internet,[a] as well as rapid transportation by air. The overriding common interest is undoubtedly the prospect of survival in the face of environmental deterioration and the menace of warfare with nuclear and other weapons of mass destruction. There can thus be little doubt that the conditions exist conspicuously (if only peoples and their national governments can be brought to see them) for world federal union.

Prejudices against federal government, widespread as they are today, are ill-founded and baseless. So far from being what many people fear and most politicians deplore – an authoritarian centralized superstate – it is the precise opposite, for it is the paradigm of devolved government, which in several contemporary states has become popular and which so many subject peoples are demanding. Genuine federalism

---

[a] The use of the internet by terrorists to disseminate propaganda, to recruit and train terrorist volunteers has now become extremely menacing; hence some form of global control over its use has become vitally necessary (not to mention the practices of hackers dissipating viruses and similar abuses).

withholds from the central government the right to intervene in the administration of the purely local affairs of its member states, reserving to the federal legislature only issues of common interest to all and such as the separate states in any case could not control, because (as now when they are sovereign) such matters are beyond the limits of their jurisdiction, and are affected by what happens and is done or left undone in other countries.

Such matters as the prevention of environmental damage, the protection of human rights, or the restraint of terrorism demand concerted action, which as we have seen cannot be achieved by agreement among sovereign states because national interests tend to conflict with the kind of action required; and even when agreement is reached there is no guarantee that it will be respected, nor is there any way of enforcing observance except sanctions involving the threat or use of military action. Accordingly, there should be some way of ensuring the implementation of measures that guarantee what is required. The only way is to abolish national sovereign claims and to establish a system of enforceable World Law, enforceable on delinquents who are individual persons (not upon sovereign states, which is impracticable without war).

World union, however, cannot be brought about through the hegemony of one super-power because other countries will not freely accept its dictate. Still less can it be imposed by conquest, because that would involve war which, almost certainly, because nations that oppose foreign domination will use every available means of resistance, would escalate into a conflict with weapons massively destructive of both prospective victor and vanquished. The federating peoples would have to embrace union by free popular decisions without duress, through referenda prior or subsequent to governmental ratification. The qualification of a federal constitution to be accepted as democratic is not how, or by whom, it is drafted, but by the action of the peoples who freely accept it.

Federalism is the one form of world union conforming to the above conditions of acceptability because it constitutionally preserves and protects the right to local self-government and individual liberty within the member states, while global concerns (problems such as global warming) are reserved to the world's federal administration, such as can neither be regulated and controlled by independent nations severally, nor be assured by international agreement between sovereign states that can never be trusted to observe their undertakings. The federal government would be empowered to enact laws that it can impose upon *individuals* without the use of excessive force (unlike the United Nations today, which cannot, except by war, enforce upon its sovereign members the resolutions of the Security Council).

World Federation is clearly the only course that can provide the means by which global problems, that can be solved only by global measures, can be effectively addressed, because it establishes the universal Rule of Law, doing away with sovereign claims of its national member states that would enable them to defy superior legislation. Accordingly, the needed remedial measures could be legally enforced worldwide, and enforced, with minimal use of force, on individuals (not on sovereign states, which is impossible without excessive destruction).

Were such a democratically constituted World Government to be established it would not automatically solve the problems so urgently crying out for resolution, but it is the indispensable precondition of any effectual remedy to global crises, if only because sovereign nations are bound by their very nature and definition to generate the conditions that exacerbate current crises.

Establishment of a world federation would, however, require the devisal and universal acceptance of a World Federal Constitution transferring sovereignty from national units to the people of the world as a whole. It would thus ensure world democracy embracing every nation within a system of world citizenship. The World Constitution would have to provide the best method of effective remedial law-making that could be offered, most probably by a tri-cameral legislature giving equal representation to national groups in one House concurrently with popular representation proportional to population density in another. It would also be salutary to include a third House, the members of which should be selected from qualified academic, social, and scientific experts, to review legislation proposed by the other two Houses, to prevent ill-considered measures from being enacted, and whose advice, in consultation, would be available to the legislators. The functions of this third House would serve to counteract the disadvantages of leaving the final decision on policies to *hoi polloi* in general elections. Whether it should have legislative power with the other two or be restricted to an advisory capacity may be left to the constituent body that frames the Constitution to decide. Possibly the best arrangement would be for it to be mainly advisory, requiring the other two Houses to reconsider ill thought-out legislation; but it could be permitted to legislate when the other two Houses failed to agree (as has from time to time occurred in

Britain when bills passed by the House of Commons have been persistently rejected by the House of Lords).

The constitution could (and should) provide for an agency to guard against the insidious infection of corruption and conflicts of interests, by setting up an Ombudsmus authorized to investigate complaints of administrative misconduct and to maintain a watchful eye against official abuse of power. It should not only deal with complaints from individuals and associations about discrimination and unjust treatment but should itself initiate investigations into suspected corruption, administrative misconduct, conflicts of interest, and the like.

To avoid the excessive influence of charismatic leaders, the Presidency of the Federal Government should not be held by a single individual, nor should it be elected from a single nationality, but should be invested in a committee of five or six, one from each of the continents. The candidates could be nominated by the House of Experts, but nominees from other international bodies (such as non-governmental organizations) need not be excluded. The members of this Presidium could be elected by a two-thirds majority of the legislative Houses sitting together, and should hold office for a term of years, with each member in turn holding the Chair for one year. Such an arrangement would guard against personality cults by preventing an undesirable concentration of power in the hands of a single individual or a single nationality, and the conduct of the Presidium should not be exempt from surveillance by the Ombudsmus.

By these means, and by no others, it would be possible to maintain the Rule of Law not just within the boundaries of independent states, but world-wide. Disputes, if they arise, between the federated nations, or between racial or religious communities, would be settled by due process of law, not by resort to force (whether terroristic or otherwise belligerent). A Bill of Rights should be enshrined in the Constitution as among its basic principles, to ensure the legal protection of civil and human freedom. With rights so ensconced, Civil Society throughout the world would be assured of the conditions of free activity and successful endeavor in the creation, through free discussion and mutual criticism, of world public opinion that would inform the legislative bodies, while at the same time, the Ombudsmus would ensure the honorable performance of responsibilities both public and private.

The traditional conception of democratic government is not altered by federation. The nature of self-government is still preserved. The legislature is still democratically elected by universal suffrage. The method of determining, at least in approximation, the General Will of the nations remains the same: namely, discussion and deliberation among the populace, within special and technical associations, between political parties, among legislators, and in the courts of law. The extent to which the defects of contemporary democratic practice can be overcome will largely depend on the provisions of the Constitution.

At the same time, it would not be immediately necessary to require the form and method of state government to be modified, if the population desired to retain its present structure, as long as the federal elections were democratic as prescribed by the World Constitution. If, for instance, a Muslim country preferred to retain the *Shariah* system of law, that would be for it to decide; even some form of Communism might be accommodated as long as it permitted popular elections to the World Parliament and observed the Federal Law on human rights (by no means an impossibility).

What the people of the world desperately need (and some actually cry out for) today is security; first against aggression and interference by foreign invaders. Under present conditions, the nations being independent and sovereign, seek to provide this for themselves by amassing armaments, which has the opposite effect because it provokes other states to do likewise and generates an arms race. Under a federal government the relations between member states would be regulated by constitutional law and any disputes between them would be settled peaceably by the courts, whose decisions could be enforced not against the states as such, but against those individuals who defied the court's judgment. Conflicts like that between the Israelis and Palestinians could be settled by legal procedures that, unlike contemporary international "agreements", can be enforced upon individuals who disobey judicial decisions, unprotected by national sovereign governments, which would no longer exist arbitrarily to ignore or defy the pronouncements of the courts. Security in such cases would be provided by the law, without resort to widespread destructive conflict.

Federal world government would do away with national arsenals of military hardware and abolish all weapons of mass destruction, for which there would no longer be any need or purpose. The global arms trade would become illegal, and any individuals suspected of or detected in the production of forbidden weapons would be immediately charged and prosecuted for committing a criminal offence.

Security against arbitrary infringement of civil and human rights would be provided by the federal administration and the Omsbudmus.

Legitimate use of force would be restricted to the World Police, who would be responsible (along with the rest of their duties) for detecting plots to commit terrorist atrocities and preventing attempts to carry them out. "War" against terrorism (apart from metaphor) is a misnomer. Like murder (individual, serial, or mass) terrorism is a crime, not an act of war. But under global federal administration terrorism would be far less likely, if it were not altogether abandoned, because the stimulating cause of terrorism would have been removed. The legitimate rights of member states would be protected by the Constitution, arbitrary interference by foreign regimes being outlawed. If in this way terrorism could be overcome the present aberrations from legitimate democratic principles would have less attraction for politicians or none at all. So security against terrorism, if any still threatened, would be forthcoming from regular democratic practices.

Security against the effects of global warming would be available from the timely action of the federal administration's enforcing suitable counteractive measures world-wide, in contrast to the tardy and inadequate proposals that have been made up to the present time and the obstruction of major powers favoring their economic interests. That such measures can be taken has been demonstrated by scientists and engineers who have told us that the technology is available to convert the use of fossil fuels by the internal combustion engine (a major source of CO^2 emissions) to hydrogen which is safely obtainable by the electrolysis of water and produces no undesirable greenhouse gas. This is only one possibility. The use of solar energy, which costs nothing once solar panels have been installed, is easily at hand; also biomass, tidal and wind power. All that is lacking is the political will and determination to undertake the conversions on a large scale and by all nations without exception.

In the conduct of the Executive, the temptation to use spin could be largely overcome, and any tendency to give way to it could be curbed by the functioning of the House of Experts giving advice and oversight to the legislative chambers. Misuse of power and conflicts of interest in administration could be vetted by the Ombudsmus. The influence of vested interests could be counteracted by the global regulation of transnational corporations and the federal control of world finance and economy. Undeveloped nations could be given credit calculated on the basis of the productive capacity of their population and territory, so that they could be freed from debt to the richer nations, and inequitable subsidies to producers in the more prosperous countries could be controlled by Federal Law, or abolished. As we have said, disputes between the member states of the federation would be settled legally without resort to military conflict. The arms trade, profiting from death and destruction, would disappear, and vast expenditures on armaments would no longer be necessary, equivalent funds becoming available for more humane objectives. Above all, the widespread fear which motivates governments at the present time would be reduced or even eliminated from world politics, giving reasonable prospect of overcoming most of our contemporary distempers.

The resolution of the problem of secularism is more difficult. It is extremely serious, even if it is not the most urgent now facing us. The alarming effects at the present time of fundamentalist influence upon national governments mainly relate to other world problems (as does belief in the literal meaning of prophesies in the Book of Revelation that make attempts to prevent global warming and other perils we now face to seem impious). As long as such influences could be excluded from the federal administration, they would have less effect. The fact that federalism protects the right of the member states to autonomy would in some degree reduce the problem, depending on the extent to which a member state is multiracial and multi-denominational. The federal government might adopt the principle of secularism constitutionally – apart from the guarantee of religious toleration – doctrinal requirements of any religious denomination being banned from its transactions, while the right to regulate matters which impinged upon religious dogma would be reserved to the member states, each of which could deal with them in its own way. The principle should be generally respected that every citizen is free to vote for any policy according to his or her conscience, whether prompted by religious doctrine or common morality, but that no organized religious denomination may directly interfere with the political process, and no administrative official should act in accordance with religious dogma in disregard of the law

This might well not be a complete or entirely satisfactory solution of the problem, because fundamentalism is so excessively unreasonable that it is difficult to imagine how it can be curbed, but its effects might in some degree be limited if its influence upon government policies could be reduced, and to ensure this again the duties of the Ombudsmus might include. It is unlikely that measures to resolve any global problem, such as the federal government alone could address, would run foul of any religious ordinance (possible exceptions being insistence on the use of condoms to prevent the spread of AIDS and the use of contraceptives to control population growth). So the issue of secularism for the federal administration should be less acute. Even so, literal acceptance of Biblical prophecies can impede efforts to address global perils if individual fundamentalists or members of extremist sects gain too close access to, and influence over, legislators or officials in the federal administration independently of legitimate representation. In a genuinely democratic political system one cannot prevent anybody holding any belief or opinion from voting for whomsoever they will; but here the danger is that extremists might catch the ear of responsible officials directly and independently of the electoral system. Possibly the House of Counselors and the Ombudsmus in a world federation could exercise sufficient vigilance to prevent such unwarranted influences, or at least reduce them to a minimum.

At the present time what prevents national governments from preserving and achieving the ideals of genuine democracy is, as has been demonstrated, the inevitable conditions and practices imposed on national sovereign states by their independent status: their need for security and their blinkered devotion to national interests. Once these obstacles have been removed, many of the defects listed in Chapters IV and V above would automatically be reduced: chauvinism is obviously one, racial intolerance might well be another and with it much religious intolerance as well; a wisely devised federal constitution could prevent personal arrogation of power to individuals (presidents and prime ministers) and the accompanying misdirected competition for party success in elections. Other forms of contemporary deficiency might well be more easily remedied, and the priority now given to purely national interests where global needs were concerned would be avoided.

The Earth is the most congenial habitat for human intelligent life in the solar system or yet discovered elsewhere in the universe. The Earth's distance from the Sun, the rate of its diurnal rotation, keeping air temperature within necessary limits (unlike the extremes suffered on other planets, such as Mercury, Venus and Mars), the presence of water and water-vapor in adequate quantities, such chemical relations as make carbon dioxide soluble (whereas kindred chemical combinations are not), and numerous other delicate adjustments of meteorological and physico-chemical relationships favourable to the existence and reproduction of life on this planet, are unique. The recent practices of mankind in industrialization and transport are disrupting this delicate balance of nature with the most dire and ominous consequences.

By and large, many people in the world seem to be unaware, or, if they are aware, not much concerned about, this dismal prospect; far less are they cognizant of what brings it about and prevents effective remedial measures from being undertaken. Further, they are for the most part ignorant of the one and only precondition of any cure for the evils now being suffered and threatening their future. If their eyes could be opened and they could see that from which they are, at present, blinkered, they might look upon world federation not just with more favour, but as what ought urgently to be embraced.

Clearly, this would only happen if they were convinced that their freedom as national groupings would be protected, which genuine federation would ensure. Under the conditions that federation can provide, such as have been outlined above, those regimes that are not now democratic might be induced to modify some of their undemocratic practices and might be persuaded to reform their systems so far as they were authoritarian and despotic by adopting more liberal practices, while the abolition of regular national armies, of nuclear or any other arsenals and massive arms manufacture would make military coups impossible. In the course of time, if not right away, genuine democracy might become universal.

Of course, the condition of such improvements and safeguards would have to be the full, fair and universal democratic representation of the peoples subject to the federal government in properly constituted legislative assemblies, as above described. If such a World Government were to be established there might be some prospect that the traditional ideals of democracy could be resuscitated and at least be approximated in practice, which is by no means the case at the present time, even in those countries that profess to be genuinely democratic.

Once the major and more urgent global problems had been dealt with, a world federal administration could turn its attention to matters of general interest that are more domesticated, such as public health and education. The present ancillary agencies of the United Nations which do much good work could be taken over by a federation of Earth and made part of its administrative structure. Education would be a very important function for the federal government to facilitate, because it is vital to improve the knowledge and judgment of the common people who are the voters and the ultimate sovereign body of the world, and it is also highly important that the ablest persons should be well trained and well informed, so that they might be available for election to the World Parliament and appointment to the world Civil Service. Such action by the federal government need not be intrusive into the educational systems devised and conducted by the state governments, but it could do much by facilitating the availability of equipment, books, scientific apparatus and the like. Advice on methods of instruction from educational experts could be made more easily and widely available. The Ombsudmus also should keep watch on the content of instruction, to make sure that it is not subversive and that extremist views are not inculcated to corrupt the youth into committing criminal terrorist acts.

Public health is another area that requires regulation and surveillance by a world authority, because diseases, especially the more infectious and contagious, do not confine themselves to separate areas and do not respect national boundaries. Already science is international, in that scientific knowledge is openly shared by all countries, although the controls on research are not universal as they ought to be, especially on biological engineering. And much more needs to be done globally to oversee the practices of pharmaceutical manufacturers, to keep the prices of beneficial drugs reasonable. It is also urgently necessary to put an end to the production and illicit sale of harmful drugs, not only to protect potential users from health hazards, but because the trade is a vicious and copious cause of violent crime.

The world economy also needs to be organized to prevent poorer countries from being hampered by protective measures taken by the more wealthy, and to facilitate equitable distribution of goods and services. Also, the use of the world's resources needs to be controlled so as to avoid exhaustion and deprivation, as well as the supply of fresh water, the use of renewable sources of energy, and the like. The rain forests must be protected and, as far as possible, resuscitated where they have been destroyed. Funds to cover costs of such measures would be plentifully provided from the savings made by the elimination of the vast expenditure now dissipated on national armaments.

If the nations of the world could be apprised of the mortal dangers now threatening the one known habitat of life, intelligent or other, and the extent to which national sovereignty prevents the adoption of the needed antidotes, they might be prepared willingly to accept federation under a global administration, as the only course of action that can save them and their peoples, along with possibly most other living species, from extinction. At all events, they cannot afford to delay, as the causes of disruption of the environment, like time and tide, are waiting for nobody, and may already be irreversible, and the human practices that accelerate them are by no means likely to be reformed unless world federation replaces national sovereignty.

Bibliography

Armstrong, Karen, *The Battle for God: A History of Fundamentalism*, NewYork,Random House, 2000.

Averni, Schlomo, *Hegel's Theory of the Modern State*, Cambridge, Cambridge University Press, 1972.

Barber, Benjamin, R. *Strong Democracy: Participatory Politics for a New Age*, Berkeley, Los Angeles, London, University of Calif Press, 1884, 2003.

Barker, Ernest, *Reflections on Government*, Oxford, Clarendon Press, 1942.

——, *Principles of Social and Political Theory*, Oxford, Clarendon Press,1951.

Bosanquet, Bernard, *The Philosophical Theory of the State*, London, Macmillan, 1925.

Field, G.C., *Political Theory*, London, Methuen, 1956.

Green, T.H. *Lectures on The Principles of Political Obligation*, London, New York, Toronto, Longmans, Green,and Co., 1924.

Hamilton, A. and Madison, J. *The Federalist*, New York, Random House.

Harris, E.E., *The Survival of Political Man: A Study in the Principles of International Order*, Johannesburg, Witwatersrand University Press, 1950.

——, *Annihilation and Utopia: The Principles of International Politics*, London, George Allen and Unwin, 1966.

——, *One World or None: Prescription for Survival*, Atlantic Highlands NJ., Humanities Press, 1993

——, *Apocalypse and Paradigm: Science and Everyday Thinking*, Westport CT, London, Praeger, 2000.

——, *Earth Federation Now! Tomorrow is Too Late*, Radford VA., Institute for Economic Democracy, 2005.

——, Hegel's Theory of Sovereignty, International Relations, and War" in *Hegel's Social and Political Thought* (D.P. Verene Ed.), Humanities Press, 1980.

——, "Hegel's Theory of Political Action", in *Hegel's Theory of Action* (D.Lamb and L.S. Stepelevich, Eds.), Humanities Press, 1983.

——, and Yunker, J.A. (Eds.) *Toward Genuine Global Governance: Critical. Reactions to "Our Global Neighborhood"*, Westport, CT., London, Praeger,1999.

Hegel, G.W.F., *Grundlinien der Philsophie des Rechts*, Leipzig, Felix Meiner, 1930;

Frankfurt-am-Main, Suhrkamp Verlag, Band 7, 1070. Trans. By T.M. Knox as *Hegel's Philosophy of Right* , Oxford, Clarendon Press, 1945, 1949, 1953.

Enzyklopädie der philosophischen Wissenschaften III, Frankfurt-am-Main, Suhrkamp Verlag, Band 10, 1970. Trans. By William Wallace, and A.V. Miller, as *Hegel's Philosophy of Mind*, Oxford, Clarendon Press, 1971.

Philosophie des Rechts: Die Vorlesung von 1819/20, Herausgegeben von Dietrich Henrich, Frankfurt-am-Main, Suhrkamp Verlag, 1983.

Die Philosophie des Rechts: Die Mitschriften Wannemann (Heidelberg 1817/18) und Homeyer (Berlin 1818/19), Herausgegeben von Karl-Heinz Ilting, Stuttgart, Klett-Cotta, 1983.

Vorlesungen über Naturrecht und Staatswissenschaft. Heidelberg 1817/18 mit Nachtragen aus der Vorlesung 1818/19 Nachgeschrieben von P. Wannermann, Herausgegeben von C. Becker, W Bonsiepen, A Gethmann, W. Jaeschke, Ch. Jamme, H-Ch Lucas, K.R. Meist, H. Schneider, mit Enleitung von O.Pöggeler. Hamburg, Felix Meiner Verlag, 1983

Lectures on the Philosophy of World History, Introduction, Trans. By H.B. Nisbet, with introduction by Duncan Forbes, Cambridge, London, New York, Cambridge University Press, 1975.

Hobhouse, L.T., *The Metaphysical Theory of the State: A Criticism*, London, 1918.

Hobbes, T., *Leviathan*, Oxford, Clarrendon Press, 1943.

Krabbe, H., *The Modern Idea of the State,* Trans. By George H. Sabine and Walter J. Shepard, London, New York, Appleton and Co., 1921.

Lamb, D. and Stepelevich, L.S. (Eds.), *Hegel's Philosophy of Action* ,Atlantic Highlands N.J., Humanities Press, 1983.

Lindsay, A.D., *The Modern Democratic State*, London, New York, Toronto, Oxford University Press, 1943, 1955.

Locke, Hume and Rousseau, *Social Contract: Essays*, with Introduction by Sir Ernest Barker, London, New York, Toronto, Oxford University Press (The World's Classics).

Lord, A.R., *The Principles of Politics*, Oxford, London, New York, Toronto, Oxford University Press, 1921.

Maritain, J., *Man and the State*, London, Hollis and Carter, 1954.

McIver, R.M., *The Modern State*, London, Oxford University Press, 1926-1950.

Mill, J.S. *Utilitarianism; On Liberty; Representative Government*, London, Toronto, J.M. Dent, New York, E.P. Dutton and Co, 1922.

Neuhouser, F., *Foundations of Hegel's Social Theory: Actualizing Freedom*, London, Cambridge, Mass. 2000.

Nicholson, P.P., *The Political Philosophy of the British Idealists*, Cambridge, New York, Cambridge University Press, 1990.

Norton, A., *Leo Strauss and the Politics of American Empire*, New Haven, London, Yale University Press, 2004.

Reyburn, H.A., *The Ethical Theory of Hegel: A Study of the Philosophy of Right*, Oxford, Clarendon Press, 1967.

Rousseau J. J., *The Social Contract and Discourses*, Trans. By G..D. H. Cole, London, J.M. Dent and sons, New York, E.P. Dutton and Co., 1946.

Scheuerman, W.L., *Carl Schmitt: The End of Law*, Lanham, New York, Oxford, Rowman and Littlefield, 1999.

Speth, J.G., *Red Sky at Morning: America and the Crisis of the Global Environment*, New Haven, London, Yale University Press, 2004, 2005.

Verene, D.P. (Ed.) *Hegel's Social and Political Thought*, Atlantic Highlands, NJ, Sussex, Harvester Press, 1980.

Index

About the Author

Errol E. Harris is John Evans Professor of Moral and Intellectual Philosophy (Emeritus) at Northwestern University and Honorary Research Fellow at the Center for the Philosophy and History of Science, Boston University. He has held named chairs at four universities and has taught and published worldwide.

Professor Harris is author or editor of 31 books in political philosophy, theory of knowledge and mind, metaphysics in relation to science, logic and the dialectical method, and the implications of holism. For many years he has specialized in the revolutionary implications of contemporary science and its social and political implications for human life.

Professor Harris is former President of both the Metaphysical Society and the Hegel Society of America and is currently a Vice-President of the World Constitution and Parliament Association. Among his many honors and awards is the Global Peace Award, presented to Professor Harris by the Provisional World Parliament at its Sixth Session in Bangkok Thailand, March 2003. He is featured in the *Dictionary of American Philosophers* and on various pages of the internet encyclopedia, *Wikipedia*.

Professor Harris has written four previous books concerning the nature of democracy, global issues, and the rational and practical foundations for a democratic, civilian earth federation: *The Survival of Political Man* (1950), *Annihilation and Utopia* (1966), *One World or None* (1993), and *Apocalypse and Paradigm* (2000). He is also co-editor of another book focusing on the arguments for democratic world law entitled *Toward Genuine Global Government* (1999).

A frequent contributor not only to scholarly journals but to world federalist publications, Professor Harris exemplifies the ideal of the engaged philosopher and intellectual, a person who devotes his considerable talent and energy to creating a decent future for human beings on our precious planet Earth.

The Institute for Economic Democracy
Global peace and sustainable development equals peace and prosperity for all
To join, email ied@ied.info
www.paypal.com/, account: ied@ied.info www.ied.info/

World Prout Assembly
Economy of the People, For the People and By the People!
To join, email gardaghista@gmail.com
www.worldproutassembly.org/

International Philosophers for Peace
Developing a just social, economic, & political basis for peace and human well-being
www.ippno.org/

Institute on World Problems
Creating a world order of peace, justice, and freedom
To join, email gmartin@radford.edu
www.worldproblems.net

Earth Rights Institute
Dedicated to securing a culture of peace and justice by establishing dynamic worldwide networks of persons of goodwill and special skill, promoting policies and programs which further democratic rights to common heritage resources, and building ecological communities.
www..earthrights.net

The Hour Money Institute for Global Harmony
Dedicated to establishing an hour of work as the money unit worldwide
www.hourmoney.org/

Global Issues (www.globalissues.org)

Rights are available for publishing in your region, in English or translations, www.ied.info/. We are available to present these concepts to your class or group. www.ied.info/.ied@ied.info

www.ingramcontent.com/pod-product-compliance
Lightning Source LLC
Chambersburg PA
CBHW071225290326
41931CB00037B/1975